# LEADING SUCCESSFUL FUNDRAISING TEAMS

CARLA MILLER

Copyright © 2017 Carla Miller

All rights reserved.

# DEDICATION

For Gill and Marion

# CONTENTS

| | |
|---|---|
| Introduction | vii |
| **Getting The Job** | **1** |
| Stepping up to lead a team | 2 |
| Securing the job (Guest chapter by Nick Billingham) | 5 |
| Defining a successful fundraising team | 8 |
| Being a great generalist | 10 |
| **Strategy** | **13** |
| Your first 90 days | 14 |
| Researching your sector | 18 |
| Strategy – how to approach it | 21 |
| OKR - Objective Key Result | 25 |
| Relationships with donors | 28 |
| **Managing Yourself** | **31** |
| Building your profile & personal brand | 32 |
| Know yourself | 35 |
| Invest in yourself | 39 |
| Your leadership style | 43 |
| Resilience | 47 |
| Productivity & prioritising | 50 |
| Delegation | 53 |
| Growth mindset | 56 |
| **Managing Your Team** | **59** |
| Creating your culture | 60 |
| Cross team working | 63 |
| Team building | 66 |
| Managing remote teams | 69 |
| Coaching your team | 72 |
| Coaching your volunteer fundraisers | 76 |
| Leading volunteers | 81 |
| Top communication tools | 84 |
| Change management | 86 |
| **Recruitment** | **89** |

# CONTENTS

| | |
|---|---|
| Succession planning | 90 |
| Attracting the best candidates | 94 |
| Holding great interviews (Guest chapter by Nick Billingham) | 98 |
| Recruiting on culture fit | 101 |
| Recruiting from the commercial sector | 106 |
| | |
| **Internal Relationships** | **109** |
| Managing upwards | 110 |
| Educating & engaging Trustees | 114 |
| Influencing your colleagues | 118 |
| | |
| **Innovation & Tools** | **121** |
| Purpose & donor engagement | 122 |
| Networking | 127 |
| Trends - transparency & technology | 132 |
| Storytelling | 135 |
| Innovation - riding the wave | 139 |
| Data and analysis (Guest chapter by Andrew Barton) | 143 |
| | |
| **Leadership Interviews** | **147** |
| Alan Gosschalk | 148 |
| Catherine Miles | 153 |
| Jenni Anderson | 164 |
| Jools Tait | 171 |
| Kate Collins | 176 |
| Kath Abrahams | 181 |
| Mark Astarita | 186 |
| | |
| **About the Author** | **191** |

# INTRODUCTION

In my early years as a fundraiser, my experience of being on the receiving end of management ranged from inspiring to downright terrible. I had managers who believed in me and developed me, and the occasional manager that made me cry and crushed my spirit. We come into this sector full of passion and wanting to make a difference, and the people who guide us and lead us often determine how much impact we can make, and how much we enjoy doing it.

My first couple of years as a manager were rocky. I made more than my fair share of mistakes but I also had great role models to learn from. And I was constantly observing and learning. What worked? What didn't and why? How do you build trust and respect and how do you tackle difficult situations? You couldn't find that information in textbooks or on training courses and how I wished you could – it would have saved me a lot of time and energy.

In the years since then I have led some talented and successful fundraising teams, working for great causes and with brilliant colleagues and friends. I only came into my own when I started leading teams. As a change maker I loved the fact that I had the ability to improve things – the way the team worked together, how we related to donors, how we packaged our work, how fundraising was viewed within the organisation. I discovered what a privilege it is to be entrusted to lead a team and how rewarding it can be.

As a consultant, I've been lucky enough to work with teams of all shapes and sizes and have studied what successful teams have in common. Often it comes down to leadership, which is what inspired me to write this book.

If you are thinking of stepping up to lead a team for the first time or to take your first Director of Fundraising role, I would encourage you to go for it. We have a shortage of talented leaders coming up through the ranks in fundraising and you could be one of them.

You will have great highs and challenging lows but you will learn and grow and will be able to unlock skills and talents you didn't even know you had. This book is mainly for you. It shares some of the lessons that I, and Fundraising Directors much more talented and experienced than me, have learnt about leadership in our time in the sector.

The chapters are bite-sized so that you can quickly gain insight, ideas or inspiration on whatever you are struggling with at the time. Just dip in and out when you want to. This isn't comprehensive guide to running a fundraising team, and in fact you won't find much content about the technicalities of fundraising. Instead, it focuses on the softer skills of leadership that can be hard to learn formally and some of the insights I've learnt along the way. This book shares how I lead teams. Like me, it isn't perfect and it won't suit everyone but I hope that there are things contained within the book that will benefit everyone and you'll find the interviews with Fundraising Directors insightful and interesting.

I've never written a book before and I don't think I knew quite what I was getting into when I came up with the idea. Over 70,000 words later, I am delighted that it is finally finished and ready to go out into the world.

I would like to say a huge thank you to the inspiring fundraising leaders that took time out of their busy schedules to participate in the interviews. Thank you so much Kath Abrahams, Jenni Anderson, Mark Astarita, Kate Collins, Alan Gosschalk, Catherine Miles and Jools Tait for your time, your insight and your honesty. Each of them has shared their personal views, which are not necessarily those of their organisations, and any errors contained within this book are entirely mine. I have also made every effort to credit the authors of any models and quotes contained within this book and will make amendments in future versions if any accreditation has been accidentally omitted.

Thank you also to Andrew Barton who kindly contributed the chapter on Data Analytics and to Nick Billingham of Charity People who contributed the chapters on Securing the Job and Interviewing. And thanks to Shivani Smith who kindly proofread the book for me.

I'd like to thank Charity People for generously sponsoring this book, making it available to the sector free of charge for 3 months in early 2017.

This book is dedicated to the memory of two fundraisers I had the honour of working closely with and who were lost to the sector and to their friends far too soon.

Gill Astarita taught me everything good I know about leading fundraising teams. She took a chance on me, she believed in me when I didn't believe in myself, she gave me a chance to shine for the first time in my career and she allowed me to be part of a fantastic and successful team at Action for Blind People. I will always be grateful to Gill for that support and the fascinating career I have enjoyed as a result. This book is my way of paying that forward.

Marion Magrath was a member of my team at Samaritans and became a wise, caring and gentle friend to our whole team and others in the organisation. We still miss you and think of you Marion.

Thank you for picking up this book (and for reading my lengthy introduction). I wish you a long and happy career changing the world as a fundraising leader.

Carla

# GETTING THE JOB

# PREPARING TO STEP UP TO LEADING A TEAM

If you're thinking of stepping up to lead a fundraising team, you're probably wondering how you prepare yourself to get the job. Here are some simple steps to get you ready…

**Understand the role**
To secure any role you need to truly understand it. Whether it's a Director of Fundraising role or heading up an income stream, each role will have its own nuances. When you've decided what role you are aiming for, review as many adverts, job descriptions and person specifications as you can for that role in the size charity you're focusing on. I mention size because a head of income stream at a top 10 charity will need some different skills than a head of the same income stream at a small charity.

Start to build your network amongst people who already have that role. Invite people for a quick coffee and ask their advice on how to prepare for the role and also what makes candidates stand out for that sort of role. Make a good impression and they will also keep their ear to the ground for potential jobs for you.

Recruitment consultants can also be a great source of information. They can review your CV and tell you how you compare to your peers for that sort of role and make recommendations. So book in a call to a recruitment consultant that you trust and that recruits at this level.

You can also use LinkedIn to look at the career paths of people who have your dream role and see what sort of experience they had and how they present themselves.

**Map your skills, knowledge and experience**
Now you know what expertise charities and recruiters are looking for in your dream role, it is time to be honest with yourself. Go through all the documents, and your notes from your meetings and calls and map out the

skills/experience/examples/personal attributes that your dream role calls for. Highlight the areas that you feel you need to develop skills, gain experience, evidence or attain knowledge and create a list. If you're not sure, ask your manager to help you identify how you could develop.

**Acquire new skills & knowledge**
It's time to create an action plan. For each of the areas in which you need to develop, identify what you're going to do and when you are going to do it. Here are some suggestions…

- Shadowing someone in the role so you can see the reality of the role and learn what it looks like to do the role really well
- Reading as much as you can around the subject – whether that's about an income stream that is new to you or about management and strategy
- Get up to speed on legislation by reading articles, referring to the Institute of Fundraising or going on a training course
- Ask your employer to send you on a training course e.g. "Finance for Non-Finance Managers" or to invest in a qualification
- Get exposure to other functions within your organisation and build relationships outside your team
- Develop yourself personally by public speaking, managing projects, chairing committees or media training
- Become a Trustee to gain an organisation-wide perspective and learn about governance

**Be proactive**
This is the thing that makes strong applicants really stand out. They've spotted problems or opportunities in their organisations and have stepped up to offer a solution. They are always thinking about how they can make things better rather than complaining about how tough their role is. They take opportunities offered to them and create opportunities themselves as well. Proactive people are offered promotions because they have demonstrated the value they bring and have done so by collaborating with colleagues rather than stepping on others to get to the top. I firmly believe you can be ambitious and be a good team player at the same time.

**Leadership**
Think about what kind of leader you are going to be and how you can start demonstrating that in your current role. Leadership goes beyond managing a team and focusing on performance. It is about creating a shared vision, taking people with you on the journey to realising that vision, managing

upwards, influencing colleagues across the organisation and thinking with an organisational perspective rather than a purely fundraising perspective.

Jenni Anderson of Haven House Children's Hospice on how she got ready to step up…

*"One of the things that I've enjoyed doing is working in organisations where you're allowed to work in places other than your day job. If your job takes up a hundred percent of your time, then where are you going to develop? You're only ever going to develop in that function. To take the next step up, you need ten percent of your time to find ways of doing different things that are going to expose you to different activities. For example, if you've never presented to a subcommittee of the board before, when you're in a director position, or even if you're in a head of team position, you will be expected to present to the board. How can you now find a way so that you can present to those people, to give you a taste of it, what questions they'll ask you, and what you actually need to present to them so that they can make sense of what you're saying?*

*Some of it is about taking steps up when opportunities arise. If your boss is off, but there's a finance committee that week, could you go in their place? Even if you don't say anything, you might learn from the conversations around you. If you want to be in a position where you're managing a team or income streams, you are going to have to step out of your comfort zones. If you're the type of person that doesn't like doing that, then don't beat yourself up about becoming a head or fundraising director. You are going to have to do things that are scary and you don't like and you're not used to and you haven't experienced before.*

*Acquire the skills you need. Like, how do you write a business plan? Have you done some benchmarking? Have you looked at your competitors? You might do that for an event, so if you look after a challenge event, I like to think you might have gone and looked at other challenge events and what they return. You've done an assessment of where your challenge event sits against other people's. You learn that by doing it. You do it, you present it, people ask you questions, they find holes in things you've written, and you know how to improve next time."*

**Recommended reading…**
"Playing Big" by Tara Mohr is great if you are looking to feel more confident about stepping up

# SECURING THE JOB

*This is a guest chapter by Nick Billingham of Charity People.*

It can be a hugely exciting time having decided you are ready for a new challenge and identified a role which seems to fit all of your key criteria, but equally, it can be quite daunting. After all, you know you are the right person for the advertised role, but how do you demonstrate that to the decision-makers?

Fundraising, like most other professions in the UK, is typically reliant on a tried and tested formula to secure new talent. A role is marketed through a job board or a recruitment agency, applications are encouraged before a shortlist is identified, and subsequently interviewed. So there are three key stages of which you are in control: finding the role, getting an interview and impressing them once you get there. Across each of these stages there are a number of things that you can do to give yourself the best possible chance to secure the job.

**Finding the role**
Luckily we work within a relatively small sector, so opportunities can usually be found on one of three job boards. As you start to look at more senior opportunities the role may not be widely publicly advertised; instead one head-hunter will hold responsibility for identifying and approaching potential candidates. This is just one more reason for working on your public profile. Make sure the people who need to know you are aware of you. This will include building relationships with a selection of recruiters - this could be the people you have worked with to recruit to your teams or it could be people recommended to you by your networks.

Beyond profile building and networking, spend some time thinking about what your dream job is. Factor in where you want to be in 5-10 years and work backwards; what does the next role need to offer me to get me there?

I often say to people that seeking a new role can be a full time occupation. It is for this reason some people will decide to hand their notice in and then start the process of applying for roles. Whether this works for you will depend on your own individual circumstances. In a lot of instances it's not a risk worth taking and if so, it is worth designating some time each week to the job search. This will ensure you have time to apply for roles that come up, but most importantly it will mean you can do justice to any applications you decide to make. You will spend this time each week doing different things. It might be enhancing your public profile or speaking to your network, or it could be honing applications and preparing for interviews. Either way, diarising some time each week will ensure you find the time to focus.

**Getting an interview**
I have written in the past about the perils of application forms; I hate the things and they feel like a bureaucratic waste of time. However, sometimes they will be a necessity and it is worth preparing for these, but hopefully you may get by with just a supporting statement! Either way you will likely be asked to present your CV and a supporting statement specific to that post. Hopefully you will be in the habit of allocating time each week to do these so either will be manageable.

It is worth recognising your CV doesn't have to be a singular document. Change it, depending on the role you are going for. Read the person specification and identify what they need and make sure you are tailoring your experience to this. The supporting statement should be personal and focused, conveying why you are interested and why you are suitable. I have found that people can often overthink this, but it really is that simple.

For Director level hires, it isn't uncommon for the recruiter to be working on a retained basis, in full partnership with the charity. If this is the case the recruiter will often hold the first round of interviews before discussing these interviews with the hiring manager.
I have met many people who assumed an invite to an interview with me would be a chat over a coffee about the job, when in reality it is running through a set of pre-agreed questions specific to the role. Whilst the questions will typically be quite top line, don't underestimate this part of the process. Perform badly or appear disinterested at this stage and you may find that is where your part in the application process ends.

**Impressing at interview**
"Fail to prepare and prepare to fail" is one of those irritating catch phrases which unfortunately rings true with interviews. As with the application

process, you will need to find time to spend time preparing. Preparation should include speaking to people who know the organisation or hiring manager you are applying to – how do they describe the people there? What are the key challenges they are facing? What are the sort of questions they typically ask at interview?

If you don't have a connection then what can you find out through social media? Personal social media accounts can offer fantastic insight into CEOs! Beyond casual social media stalking, you will certainly need to have spent time thinking over key experiences that will likely be relevant to the role you are going for.

Competency based interview questions are common and it is worth identifying the key competencies you expect them to test and ideally having examples to talk through for each.
It is worth noting some examples will fit a number of competencies so you don't necessarily need a bank of 15 examples!

The key with any interview is to try and enjoy the process. It may involve an assessment centre with role plays; it probably will involve a presentation, but whatever is included, try and enjoy it and relish the challenge in front of you. In Britain, it seems to be natural to underplay previous achievement, so it might be worth running through tangible successes before an interview with a friend/family member. Balance is the key here; you want to ensure the interview panel are made aware of your outstanding historical achievements, but you don't want to come across as arrogant. If you have pre-planned and practiced, you should be able to deliver this in the right tone.

It is highly unlikely you will meet every single one of the assessment criteria for the post. This is ok and quite common. I always think it is worth recognising this and countering it by being ready to talk through an example of overcoming a knowledge/experience gap. This will demonstrate self-awareness and problem solving! As you reach the conclusion of the interview, it is worth having a strong close pre-planned. Genuine enthusiasm and confidence goes a really long way here.

Finally, think about the sort of questions you are going to ask when prompted. There are lots of suggestions online for these but try and think about what is genuinely important for you. The interview should be a two way process and you should be using it to identify if an opportunity and organisation is right for you as much as the other way round.

# DEFINING A SUCCESSFUL FUNDRAISING TEAM

You're reading this book because you're interested in leading a successful fundraising team but how do we define successful? I asked some inspiring fundraising leaders for their thoughts…

**Alan Gosschalk of British Asian Trust (and previously Scope)…**

*"I think they need to be always taking decisions based on what's in the best interest of the charity with respect to the supporters, working as a team and not be too insular in terms of who they're approaching and how. Seeing supporters as people in the round is vital. Relationship development is really important, both internally and externally, and good teams ensure that they're going the extra mile. Ultimately we want to be people's favourite charity so what is it that we can do to make them feel special about Scope and what Scope achieves, the information they're getting, and how they're engaged?"*

**Jools Tait of BEN…**

*"A successful fundraising team for me needs to know and understand the brand, the organisation, the cause. They need to be able to consistently give a coherent 5 minute elevator pitch about what the organisation stands for. They need to have real clarity and understanding, about what the organisation does, but also what their role is within it.*

*A successful team also needs to have licence to be creative, take their own initiative, take risks. So I think, one thing that stops fundraisers being as successful as they can be is the, 'oh no, better not do that, because we haven't sought permission to do it' and 'well I'll go back and check with my supervisor'. Just be a little bit more ballsy, a little bolder. Be proud of what you do, have the confidence. A successful team always has confidence.*

*Fundraisers need to have the will to act on their own initiative and, I really think this one is really important, not be afraid or held back because they think they will make a mistake and they'll be berated for it or that they'd have to explain it. It's that freedom to fail. Because you know what, the worst case scenario, it doesn't work out then nothing lost, nothing gained."*

## Kate Collins of Teenage Cancer Trust...

*"It's a fundraising team that's making the right amount of money for the organisation. And doing it in a way, and this is particularly pertinent at the moment in terms of in the sector, that isn't irritating people and is congruent with the values of the charity.*

*I believe that a successful fundraising team needs to be really behaviourally aligned. But it's not necessarily about standardising everything. If you donate to Teenage Cancer Trust you might get a different 'thank you letter' depending on which way you give money to us but fundamentally you'll get thanked and you'll get (or you should get!) something that is friendly and warm.*

*What makes things work at Teenage Cancer Trust, might not work at another charity because their culture might not be as strongly driven as ours is by relationships, by being a family, by looking after each other, by teenage spirit and by eating far too much cake. In other places I've worked – and this isn't a judgement either way - some of the things that work here would be really weird behaviour, out of step with what those charities do.*

*So here a successful fundraising team is a team that really cares deeply about each other, cares deeply about supporters, that pitches in across teams, and celebrates success and has fun.*

*And actually playing and laughing is really important at Teenage Cancer Trust. We are a young organisation, we look after young people. And I would very much hope that we are raising money through relationships in a way that fits with the organisation."*

To me a successful fundraising team...
- is a happy team where people genuinely like each other
- is brilliant at engaging donors in the cause, listening and creating a clear vision of a better future
- is great at relationships – with donors, with other teams and with each other
- exceeds financial targets
- celebrates success and honestly acknowledges failures
- sets high standards for itself, aims for excellence and constantly learns and innovates

Have a think about how you would define a successful fundraising team and make a list or a description. Now compare that to your team and map how you're going to get there (or keep it up).

# BECOMING A GENERALIST

When you step up to lead a team that includes fundraisers from different specialisms you have to make a shift from being a specialist in your area of fundraising to becoming more of a generalist.

Traditionally managers have the answers to their team's issues but you'll be managing people who know more about their area of fundraising than you do. You may not have previously faced the challenges that are specific to their role.

For example as a Corporate Fundraising Manager who steps up to lead a Corporate, Trusts and Statutory team, you'll find yourself dealing with the political landscape, onerous reporting and a lot of detail rather than the pitches and partnerships that you've been good at. So how do you add value in that situation? How do you even know if the person you're managing is good at their job? How do you manage and motivate people who may have different communications styles or priorities to you? How do you establish credibility as their manager?

When you first became a line manager, you learnt a new way of working. Now it's time to evolve again and become a generalist. Here are some of the factors involved in being a great generalist…

**Build trust and mutual respect**
Trust is key to your relationships with your direct reports and you gain trust through honesty and making sure that your words and actions align. I have always found it helpful to be upfront about the extent of the knowledge and experience I have of their area and recognise their expertise. Starting from a place of mutual respect is also a good idea i.e. you work from the assumption that they are great at their job and they work from the assumption that you are great at yours.

### Set clear boundaries
Ultimately you are responsible for the performance of your team and so you will want to have some influence over their activity, even though you are still learning about it. Explain that you will be held accountable (so you're not going to be totally hands off) and are keen to understand as much as possible and to add value. Set clear boundaries about what you need to know and be involved in.

### Understand what they need from you
When you're managing people who are themselves managers or heads of teams, their needs will be very different from junior team members from the same specialism as you. If they're performing well they may well resent you trying to 'manage' them. So find out what help they need from you and get really good at delivering that. It might be improving relationships with the programmes team, pushing through change internally or some of your time to attend key meetings but unless you ask, you won't know how best to support and lead them.

### Be their champion
The best leaders and managers are champions of their team. They negotiate internally, they fully support their team members, they ensure that those doing the work are given the credit and they help raise the profile of those who work for them.

### Agree objectives and KPIs
Make sure, even if you don't yet understand all of the detail, that you know exactly what you expect of your direct reports and so do they. An objective setting session will also help you to understand what the variables that can and cannot be controlled are for each income stream and how to identify good and poor performance.

### Take a coaching approach
A coaching approach can be a great way to approach managing specialists. It assumes that people have the ability to come up with their own great solutions if you ask the right questions and provide them with the support and confidence to do so. It's empowering for the person being coached and means you don't always have to have all the answers.

### Get great at internal negotiation
The higher you rise in an organisation, the more important this becomes. Being able to influence change in other teams or departments is crucial to success if you're going to help your team perform at their best.

**Be aware of your bias**
In all likelihood, your specialism involves approaching tasks in a certain way. Some income streams require huge attention to detail, others need visionary big picture thinking. In some areas, being brilliant with words is crucial, in others it's all about the numbers. You are likely to have different strengths and aptitudes to those you manage and it's important that, as well as bringing your perspective, you learn to think like they do and understand why they approach things in the way that they do.

**Learn and fill in the gaps in your knowledge**
Learn as much as you can about the income streams that you are now responsible for. Identify what they need from the organisation to be successful. Attend events and read relevant blogs. The more you know, the more you will be able to support your team to perform well.

# STRATEGY

# YOUR FIRST 90 DAYS

You only get one chance to make a first impression and as a Fundraising Director you have a lot of people to make a good impression with.

Your team will be anxious to know what your management style is and whether you're planning any big changes. Your fellow directors will be assessing how you fit into the leadership team. Your CEO will be looking for evidence that they made the right decision in hiring you and will want to hear your assessment of the fundraising function as it stands. Trustees will be keen to see results and you'll want them to feel that they can trust you. Volunteers will want to know that they are valued and key donors will want to feel safe in your hands, valued and inspired by the reasons you joined the charity.

So the pressure is on. That's why it's good to have a 90 day plan for yourself which sets out what you want to achieve. Your plan will help you focus on your top priorities. It will help you feel like you've achieved something when your days seem full of inductions and information overload. It shows your CEO your structured approach for getting to know the organisation and it sets expectations for when you'll be making key decisions.

Your approach to your new role will depend on what the organisation needs and also on your natural style. An organisation in crisis needing a quick turnaround will need a quicker assessment and a more radical change plan than one that is performing well. Make sure that you and your CEO are agreed on expectations for your first 3 months so that you're not accused of either creating instability or making insufficient impact. The onus is on you to adapt your approach to suit the culture of the organisation. Be sure to communicate your thinking style to your CEO too so that they know how you like to approach decision-making.

You can format your 90 day plan in a way that works for you and you'll find lots of templates on the internet. I usually break mine down into 3 stages…

**By 30 days – observe, meet and learn**
- **Who?** Who do I need to meet as a priority? Who are our supporters? Who are our volunteers? Who are our Trustees?
- **What?** What does the organisation deliver? What does the budget look like? What are the existing priorities? What is the organisational culture like? What are our competitors doing? What's our USP?
- **How?** How are things done around here? How are we raising money? How do we communicate? How are decisions made?
- **Why?** Why do our donors support us? Why do my team like working here? Why do volunteers get involved?

Key output – contacts made, reflect back to CEO what you see

**By 60 days – assess and audit**
- **Team** – is there a strong sense of team within the department and individual teams? Is there much cross-team working? How about competition or tension over donor funds? Are they all clear what is expected of them? Is everyone performing well? Are there any personal issues you need to be sensitive about? Are managers and leaders sufficiently knowledgeable and good managers?
- **Donor relationships** – how do donors feel about the organisation? Which donors have the greatest potential? What is the approach to stewardship and the donor journey?
- **Income streams** – does the income stream mix make sense? What does it look like in a Boston matrix? Where is there room for improvement? Which income streams have the greatest potential? What's missing and what's not working?
- **Process** – are the processes around fundraising effective? Is risk being well managed? Are we compliant with regulations?
- **Infrastructure** – are relationships good with the rest of the organisation? Is the wider organisation holding back fundraising in any way? Who are the influencers that you need to build strong relationships with? Are Trustees engaged in fundraising?
- **Culture** – is there a shared team vision or purpose? How would you describe the culture? How is fundraising seen within the organisation?
- **Projects & packaging** – are there enough fundable projects? Are we getting full cost recovery? Do we package projects and activities as effectively as possible? Is the balance of restricted and unrestricted funds right for the organisation?

Key outputs – an understanding of the challenges, opportunities, strengths and weaknesses of the organisation for fundraising purposes. Start to build key relationships internally and externally. Start adding value to the fundraising and wider activities of the organisation through insight and getting involved.

**By 90 days – recommendations and action**
- Personal objectives for first 6 months & year
- Share analysis with CEO including SWOT, Boston matrix and assessment of performance of income streams
- Discuss organisational readiness to fundraise and start to influence changes
- Thoughts on budget and reforecast if required
- Start to lead on key relationships with donors
- Fully participate as a director of the organisation

Kath Abrahams of Diabetes UK talks about her first 90 days in the job…

*"Your first 90 days is the opportunity when you've still got fresh eyes and one of the things that I've tried to do here coming into a new role, is to start it very much by learning and listening.*

*I think there's definitely a piece around trust. I develop my ideas through talking to other people. Building a sense of what I think about the situation, rather than coming in with a very fixed view. I've got some principles that I'd like to work and I suppose there's something also about making sure I don't wait too long and that I send some signals early.*

*I'm now 6 weeks in and I've just shared my early thoughts about where I think we need to try and get to with our executive team and my senior management team. I've positioned it to them very much as "this is what I think we need to be trying to do. If that's right, these are the main things I suggest we need to do to them in this. I've based this on the conversations that I've had with you over the last 6 weeks. Is this in the right ballpark?"*

*We're now creating, co-creating the plan for the big steps that we need to take to get there."*

Jenni Anderson of Haven House Hospice on how to approach your first 90 days in the role…

*"First do an assessment; you look at where the gaps are, you look at the improvements that are already there, you look at what's going really well, and then you reflect on*

*whether you need to make any changes or not. You are either the type of person who does that immediately, or, you maybe do it over six months to a year. Your personality will drive how you approach those things. I don't think there is a right way, and hopefully if you're going into a new job, you've been given a heads up about what they would like you to do, rather than you're just faced with the question "Is this a 'I've got to change this around really quickly' type job, or is this a 'this team is doing really well and we just want to grow by X percent each year?' job? Hopefully you'll have been able to prepare for this in advance."*

**Further reading...**
The First 90 Days by Michael Watkins

# RESEARCHING YOUR SECTOR

When you move to a new organisation, or take on more responsibility within your current organisation, it offers you a great opportunity to take a step back from the day-to-day and look more broadly at the sector.

## Understand your marketplace

It is a good idea to regularly scan your marketplace for new developments. You can do this at a number of levels. What are the charities that are similar to you doing in terms of service delivery, fundraising and marketing? How about the other charities that your donors support? Also look at the largest charities and see what they're doing and the same for newer entrants who are making a big noise or doing things differently. It is also a good idea to look internationally, particularly for global charities and at other sectors such as education and the arts if you're a mainstream social welfare charity.

You are looking for innovation, successes, problems, return on investment ratios, donor lists, great relationship fundraising, integration of campaigning and fundraising – anything that you can learn from. Look also at branding and how you would characterise the different brands in your sector. Are you the young upstart? The established institution? Or is your place in the market a bit indistinct?

## Benchmarking

It is hugely helpful to be able to benchmark your overall performance and the performance of your various income streams against other charities. It can provide useful management information and reassure Trustees. Having said that, every charity is different and has different assets and challenges as well as different historical investment into income streams. If you're new to major donors, your ROI will be very different from a team with 20 years head start on you. And legacies have a great ROI but take years to kick in. You know this but make sure that your CEO and Trustees do too, especially if they love to talk about ratios.

## Sharing ideas and challenges

One of the benefits of networking with your peers is to gather benchmarking information and other updates on what is happening in the sector. As Jenni describes below, the hospice movement is a great example of collaboration between charities. The Institute of Fundraising Special Interest groups are really useful for income streams and there are a number of one-off events and information gatherings for Fundraising Directors, mainly run by consultancies. I really recommend taking the time away from your desk to go and be inspired and encouraged by meeting with your peers and sharing ideas and challenges.

## Case study: How Jenni Anderson approached researching the sector when she joined Haven House Children's Hospice

What is lovely about the hospice sector is that we're very good at helping each other learn and develop. We're very good at sharing. Regardless of location, if you're looking for evidence of a particular idea, someone will say "I know somebody who's done that" and you can have an honest chat with them. When I started at Haven House, I did quite a lot of fact finding and the sector was very accommodating.

I do also like seeing how growth models and theories can be put into practice. One of my favourite models is Ansoff's Growth Matrix. You can always make improvements to your existing products in your existing markets but if you want to grow, you've often got to go in a different direction. It also encourages you to look at your competitors to identify your gaps. So we analysed what other hospices were doing, what sectors or activities they were working in and where they were seeing a good return.

As an example, Haven House joined a hospice lottery partnership in the months before I started. For the first year, we grew our player base and three years later, we're at 7,000 players. It isn't an innovative fundraising idea, but it was innovative for us at the time.

Retail was another growth area. We had one shop and our long-term plan is to open seven shops. We're now at four. We can use our shops to analyse our growth – for example does a shop impact positively on supporter growth? And we can see (using postcodes and the wonders of Google Maps) that it does.

Before we embarked on our shop expansion plans, I visited hospices and other charities that had 20 shops and asked, "When you were opening your 20 shops, what did you do?" It was important to our Trustees that we had done our research, as retail can be a huge financial risk for a charity. Learning from others helped us to develop our plan.

I spent some time reviewing all the benchmarking reports for the sector, and went through them line-by-line comparing our performance. I would recommend this for anyone going into a new role, either at Director or Head of department level. It's still important to talk to people though. You don't just sit at desk with a few reports and then pull out your plan and say "This is what we're going to do".

There are still many things that other charities do, that I look at and think "We could so easily do that. How are we going to do that?" I try and encourage my team to look at what others are doing. If we're a £4 million charity and there are £10 million hospices out there, what are those £10 million pound hospices doing that we're not doing? How do we get there?

# STRATEGY – HOW TO APPROACH IT

Writing a fundraising strategy for the first time, whether for a team or a department, can be a bit daunting but actually it is a brilliant way to clarify your thoughts, engage your team in future thinking, have important conversations with colleagues and set priorities.

A strategy is simply your plan for the future. It considers…
- **Where are you now?**
- **Where do you want to be?**
- **How are you going to get there?**

Depending on what is going on for your organisation, your fundraising strategy might be for 3-5 years or it could just be one year if the charity is going through a lot of change or you have started at the end of an existing organisational strategy period. What is crucial is that your fundraising strategy is created in alignment with the organisational strategy and the other areas of your team and organisation.

**Where are you now?**
Before you can plan the future, you need to have an accurate understanding of your current situation. It is good to do this thinking collectively as a fundraising team so you can look at the bigger picture, and also for individual teams to do it together in more detail. Often this is done as part of an away day, in which case be sure to circulate questions beforehand so that everyone can come prepared, particularly those who like to take their time to think about things rather than come to an immediate conclusion. Asking people to come with their thoughts is also a good way of making sure that everyone contributes and that everyone feels their contribution is valued. The perspective of a junior staff member is often surprising and very valuable for heads of teams who are usually thinking about different issues.

You might want to try these approaches to auditing your current fundraising activity…
- Review **performance against budget and against objectives**
- **Review of the year**/previous year's successes, challenges and what you've learnt – it can be good to ask everyone to share their personal review and their perspective on the team's performance as a whole
- **Seek feedback** from donors, volunteers and colleagues on what you've done well and where you could improve
- **Ask each other how you've worked together this year** – what's worked well and where have there been tensions? How were decisions made to resolve those tensions? Does everyone feel valued and able to contribute?
- **Use models to review the performance of your products** such as Ansoff's Matrix and product life cycles
- Undertake a **SWOT** (Strengths, Weaknesses, Opportunities & Threats) analysis, including feedback from other teams
- Undertake a **PESTLE** (Political, Economic, Social, Technological, Legal and Environmental) analysis to understand the external environment that you are operating within. Fundraising never happens within a vacuum and the environment for fundraising is changing a lot at the moment.
- Look at what **competitors and high growth charities** in the sector are doing, particularly those that were the same size as your charity a few years ago.
- Do a **risk analysis** to identify the areas where your income (or other key resources like fundraisers) could be vulnerable.

**Where do you want to go?**
Next, you need to think about what you want to achieve. Again, an away day is a great way to do this collectively so that the team feels a real sense of ownership over the strategy. It is hard to engage people in a strategy when they don't have any real say in it or when it is presented as a fait accompli. Don't tell people you're consulting them if you have no intention of taking their feedback on board – that is presenting, not consulting and it really alienates people. I always start these sessions with a brainstorm and then narrow it down to more realistic options from there.

Things to consider include…
- **What are we raising funds for** and **how much does the organisation need us to raise**?
- **How much do we think we could raise** based on what we know

about past performance and future plans? **How could we increase that** with additional investment or other input such as resources, a CEO who is happy to ask for money etc.?
- Which areas of fundraising have the **greatest potential for growth**? What could they look like in a year/3 years?
- How do we want our donors and volunteers to feel about us?
- How do we want to feel at the end of the year/3 years?
- **What are our colleagues planning** that we can utilise for fundraising e.g. campaigns, projects, partnerships?

From there you can create some **fundraising objectives** for your team which summarise your key priorities and against which progress can be measured. Make sure that you are using the same structure for your objectives and strategy as the rest of your organisation.

## How do we get there?

This is when we get into the detail of your plans and budgets. The areas you'll be thinking about are…
- **Objectives** for each income stream with associated **budgets and cash flow**
- What **activities** are required in order to achieve those objectives?
- How are we **dependent on other teams** to achieve our objectives and how they are dependent on us? It's good to formally consult relevant colleagues so that all essential activity is factored into plans.
- What **resources** are required?
- How will you **package and market** any new activities? What **collateral** do you need e.g. brochures, Case for Support?
- What is your **timeframe**? It can be good to summarise this as a month-by-month **action plan** that shows where the times of pressure may be.
- How will you know that you've achieved your goals? Make sure that you have **KPIs** that are clear and measurable and that you are **monitoring progress** quarterly.

I recommend reviewing progress against strategy on a quarterly basis at a team meeting so that you can reforecast as required and change anything that isn't working. Plans are great but circumstances change and sometimes things don't work or perform better than expected and it is helpful to take time to review and amends plans with that new information.

Mark Astarita of British Red Cross on his approach to strategy…

*"I know some people refer to their strategy all the time, but it's not the way I operate. I almost always know where we are going, but I need to make sure everyone else knows where we are going too. So yes our strategy is highly visible but we tend to live and breathe it rather than use it as a totem pole.*

*People like to think it's all about the strategy and it's all written down like the gospel. I believe it's about having people who adjust daily, respond to the insight they gather and adjust to their environment. I'm surrounded by hundreds of years of fundraising experience. All my senior managers have been with me for nigh on ten years, and just get it. They don't make the mistakes that they did when they were a lot younger because like me they've already been there, done that and made mistakes in the past.*

*None of our great successes at British Red Cross were delivered by one big decision. It was more about the decisions being taken everyday that myself, and my managers in particular, knew were the right decision to take that day and next week and next month. Cumulatively they add up to a big thing. So this idea it is one big thing bothers me - I think it is a product of our cumulative actions. Many of the things that have made the biggest difference grew from tiny shoots and featured strategically. For example, growing regular giving might be the big goal but the path to that goal had many variations and products and not all were apparent at the outset."*

## Recommended reading…

If you are in your first head of team or Director of Fundraising role, I would recommend reading Fundraising Management by Adrian Sargeant and Elaine Jay which has a structured and detailed approach to planning and addresses each income stream in detail.

# TEAM OBJECTIVES

Fundraising strategies often have two downfalls that mean that they aren't as useful on a day to day basis as they could be. Firstly, as a rather large document, once your fundraising strategy is written there is a danger that it sits on a shelf (albeit a virtual shelf these days) and isn't referred to again other than the odd mention of strategy at meetings. Secondly, most fundraising strategies contain so many objectives that they cannot all be remembered and those objectives are rarely prioritised. That is why I was really interested to come across this idea of OKRs (Objectives & Key Results), which is widely used in the corporate world, in particular in technology companies.

I highly recommend reading the short book **"Radical Focus – Achieving Your Most Important Goals with Objectives and Key Results** by Christina Wodtke. I could only find it on Amazon as it doesn't seem to be published in the UK. It is a fairly short book that shows you how OKRs work in practice but in the meantime I am going to attempt to summarise the principle for you in this chapter.

The key benefit of OKRs is that they enable the whole department or team to align behind the same objective for a period of time, making it more likely that you will reach that goal and preventing you from losing focus. The main principles behind OKRs are:

1. Set inspiring and measurable goals
2. Make sure you and your team are always making progress towards those goals as a priority
3. Use a framework that makes you all remember what you are trying to accomplish and keep each other accountable.

**Setting Objectives & Key Results**
The Objective is what you want to do. Objectives are a **single sentence** and are **inspiring** – they should make you want to leap out of bed in the

morning. Objectives are set as **part of your annual strategy** and align with your organisational vision. Each team has one objective per quarter and it should be **achievable within that timeframe**. The best objectives focus on things that your team can **control**.

Key Results are how you know if you have achieved your objective – they **quantify your objective**. Ask yourself – **how would we know if we met our objective?** Key Results involve numbers and should be **stretching**. It is typical to have **3 Key Results** and they can measure things like growth, engagement, revenue, performance and quality – anything you can quantify in some way.

In the corporate world OKRs are **stretch goals**, used to improve performance and think bigger. A typical OKR might have a 50:50 chance of being achieved – but even if you
don't achieve it, you will have pushed yourselves further as a team than you do currently. I would suggest taking a slightly more moderate approach in fundraising, only because the consequences of failing to meet financial targets are greater in our sector. You might want to start more cautiously and then get bolder as the team gets used to working with OKRs. They are a great way to build energy and motivation around some key goals.

Here is an example of OKRs across a year for a major donor team…

| Quarter | Objective | Key Results |
|---|---|---|
| Quarter 1 | Recruit an incredible Development Board | 80% of invitations to join Board accepted
10 Board Members recruited |
| Quarter 2 | Make our annual donor dinner the best yet | All seats sold
£1 million raised
30% of attendees new to us |
| Quarter 3 | Successfully launch new campaign | Existing donors bring 100 new prospects to launch event
Lead gift of £750,000 secured
5 new donor giving £50k+ |
| Quarter 4 | Build amazing relationships with our major donors | 75% of donors met in person or visited project
20% of donors introduce us to new contacts |

## Cascade OKRs

OKRs then cascade down the team and each team's OKRs for that quarter are focused on what they need to do to help the overall Fundraising Team reach its OKRs. So if your overall Fundraising Team objective for this quarter is "Turning our supporters into passionate advocates for our charity" then in the corporate team the objective might be "Make our account management of corporate supporters the best in the sector" and a community fundraising objective might be "Create a team of community ambassadors".

## Weekly progress updates

Weekly updates on progress by each team keep OKRs front of mind. The author of Radical Focus lays out a very comprehensive structure for these meetings but to start with I suggest that you stick to:

- Progress on last week's top 3 priorities
- Top 3 priorities for this week
- Projects/activities for the next month (so that you can see what other teams are planning)

These could be shared weekly at very focused team meetings or on a weekly email update and then you can check in at a monthly team meeting.

## Implementing OKRs

You could also agree how you celebrate if you achieve your OKRs and how you debrief and learn each time. OKRs can take a while to get the hang of and you can adapt them to work for your team. Even if the only thing you get from this concept is the idea to focus the team on one shared objective each quarter that would improve the quality of your fundraising, I think that could add a lot of value.

You can also set yourself personal OKRs. If, like me, you start the year with a long list of things you'd like to do, see and achieve, then the focus of OKRs means that you can really get things done. This quarter for example my objective was to get this book written and I have set aside other things to make sure that it happened.

## Recommended reading...

"Radical Focus – Achieving Your Most Important Goals with Objectives and Key Results by Christina Wodtke.

# RELATIONSHIPS WITH DONORS

Obviously fundraising is all about relationships with donors but in this chapter I would like to focus on how you, as a fundraising leader, approach relationships with donors. I'll be primarily aiming this at Fundraising Directors but the same principles can be applied if you manage an income stream.

**Change your focus**
As a Fundraising Director you're often thinking about the financial side of fundraising. Ultimately you are responsible for the team reaching its targets and ensuring that the organisation has enough funds to carry out its work effectively. You're tracking weekly figures and looking in-depth at the budgets monthly to see what's going well and what isn't. You're also motivating your team to reach their targets and celebrating when the money comes in as planned.

You've got money on the mind. And so has your team. And there is nothing wrong with that – your team name is, after all, fundraising. But it can overshadow the importance of supporters. Without supporters you have no money and yet there are times when supporters can appear to be a means to an end. The idea of that is no doubt horrifying to you because you do genuinely care about your supporters. But take a step back and think about those times when you have been so focused on reaching your end of year target or improving retention rates that you've temporarily forgotten that behind it all are a lot of people. People with needs of their own. People who want to make a difference. People that possibly aren't all feeling loved and valued by your organisation right now.

Kath Abrahams of Diabetes UK on donor care…

*"I think some of it is about getting the basics of human interaction right. Everybody we're dealing with, however they support us, are all individual human beings. In the current environment that is rightly focused on compliance, let's also make sure that the*

*relationships that people have with us feel authentic and that they can trust us. Many of our supporters either have diabetes themselves or it has impacted one of their loved ones. We absolutely have a responsibility to make sure their experience is one that feels congruent and relevant."*

I would like to encourage you to put relationships with supporters up at the top of your agenda alongside income. If you improved your relationships with donors by even 10% that would no doubt have a positive impact on income too so there is a strong business case for doing so. But it would also bring more joy to your team as well as your donors.

Fundraisers are natural relationship-builders but when their primary measurement of success is income then it becomes the priority. So think about how you are measuring success. Think about what you celebrate. Think about how you communicate the work of your team internally. But most importantly think about how you can give your donors the sense of impact and being part of something that they want. Not that <u>you</u> want so that you can increase their donation or retain them as a donor, but the relationship that <u>they</u> want.

I love how Catherine Miles approached relationship management at Anthony Nolan and now at Breast Cancer Now. You can read about that in her interview later in this book. How could you apply those principles in your team? What would it look like if everyone was focused more on relationships than income streams and products?

**When you start**
Your first 3-6 months in post are a great time to talk to donors about their relationship with your charity and gather important insight and feedback. If, as a new Director, you ask major donors, corporate supporters and legacy pledgers some smart questions, then they can be honest in their feedback without fear of upsetting you. You can also listen without feeling defensive, which will make it much easier to take what they are saying on board.
So schedule in meetings with key donors as a priority in your first few months. Tell them that you're hoping to understand more about your supporters and find out if you can improve their experience of supporting the charity.

When you meet with them, and before you rush into your questions take some time to get to know them and to say thank you for their support. Then find out why they give to your charity – how did they hear about you? What appealed about this particular cause or organisation? Which area of your work is most interesting to them?

Ask them about their experience of supporting you. What has worked well for them? What do they like about the communications they have from your team? Do they feel valued? Do they feel informed? Are you sharing the sort of information they want to receive? Are you communicating enough? Or too much? How would they rate their relationship with your organisation out of 10? Why? What could you do to improve that?

You could carry out a similar exploration using focus groups for donors. When you've spoken to a range of donors, you can then analyse the feedback that you have gathered and identify ways that you can improve your approach to donor relationships as a team.

**Your own portfolio?**
In some organisations Fundraising Directors have their own portfolio of donors and a target of their own. In others Fundraising Directors have personal relationships with key donors but no personal target. And in a few of the larger organisations the Fundraising Director mainly deals with internal issues and rarely deals with donors directly. Each charity and individual will have their own needs and preferences.

As Fundraising Director, I see my role as supporting the team, taking overall responsibility for the income target, engaging with key supporters and stepping in to help where I am needed. I've always acted as an Account Director on major partnerships, projects and relationships – attending key meetings, dealing with issues that crop up, thanking them and getting hands on when needed at gala dinners, sporting events etc. Not having a personal target has freed me up to do that and keeps me neutral in decisions about where income sits. Even when I'm making the ask, I am doing so for a team target rather than a personal one. I think it is really important to stay connected to donors and to be available to them and the team when issues crop up.

What's most important is that you think carefully about how you can best add value to donors and to your team when it comes to targets and relationship management. Play to your strengths but make the needs of the donors a priority.

Mark Astarita of British Red Cross on relationships with donors…

*"In our fundraising team we are always very aware that donors have got plenty of other choices for their giving. It's my colleague Richard Verden who always says, "We need to be perpetually petrified that people decide not to give to us." There is something about that very forceful statement that no one has to give to us."*

# MANAGING YOURSELF

# BUILDING YOUR PROFILE & PERSONAL BRAND

**Why it matters**
It can be hard to stand out from the crowd. When you apply for jobs you are just one of many candidates with similar experience so you can't be sure you'll even be shortlisted. Imagine if the charities you admire were actively approaching you for a job because they'd heard you were great. That's what building your profile and your personal brand can do for you.

**What is a personal brand?**
Ask any expert and they'll tell you that a corporate brand is much more than a logo or strapline. It's the whole experience that people have of an organisation. And it has to be authentic. The same principle applies for your personal brand – it's about how you want people to think and feel about you, however they come into contact with you.

For example if you want to be seen as professional then you need to make sure that professionalism comes across in how you deal with colleagues and supporters, how you answer the phone, how you act when you're stressed out and your social media profiles. We've all heard the urban myth of the job candidate who treats a random person terribly en route to their interview only to discover that the 'random' person is actually the interviewer. It's also why I make sure that I treat receptionists with the same warmth and respect as I treat CEOs – it's all part of your first impression and how you treat people who can't help you says a lot about you as a person.

**Know where you're headed**
To build an effective personal brand you need to know what you are trying to achieve. Do you want to head up the best corporate partnerships team in the sector? Become a Director of Fundraising or CEO one day? Become a consultant or work for a funder? Or simply have the best pick of jobs at the

level you're at now? You need to be clear on that so that you can map out your strategy.

You need to decide…

- **WHAT** you want people think about when they think of you
- **HOW** you want people to feel about you
- **WHO** you want to raise your profile with

Let's start with some thinking about your personal brand. Grab a pen and paper and answer these questions…

- **What are your values at work?** For example is it important to you to be honest? To be helpful? To be successful? To be a leader? To be thorough? Inspiring? Popular? Expert? Team player?
- **If that's hard then consider what you'd hate people to think about you and then reverse it.** For example I would hate people to think I was taking the credit for their work so integrity and championing others are important values for me.
- **What words would you like people to use to describe you?**
- **What words do people already use to describe you?**
- **What direction do you want your career to head in?**
- **How do you want people to feel about you?**
- **How do you want people to feel about themselves after spending time with you?**

The answers to those questions should give you some ideas about **WHAT** you want people to think about you. Distil that down into a few words or sentences so that you can keep them front of mind.

Now onto the **WHO**. Who are you trying to influence? Is it your colleagues? Recruiters? Future employers? Future clients if you're thinking of being a consultant?

Grab your notebook again and…

- **Note the top 3 target audiences** that you want to influence at the moment (and then update it in the future if your focus changes).
- **Write down where these target audiences get their information from.** This relates back to WHAT you want to achieve. If you're looking to establish yourself as a thought leader

in corporate partnerships then where are your target audiences getting their information about corporate partnerships from? If you're looking for your next job as a Head of Trusts, where do the existing Head of Trusts and Directors of Fundraising spend time?

Now you know what impression you want people to have of you and who you want to impress you can make a plan of action.

## Internal profile raising

- Volunteer for working groups, social committees etc. to build your relationships outside of your team
- Look for opportunities to improve on the ways things are done and offer to help
- Be sure to thank and raise the profile of anyone that helps you. For example if the Director of Programmes takes time out of their day to meet one of your donors and a gift is then made, be sure to update and thank them and share the credit with them.
- Share your long term objectives with your line manager and get them on board

## External profile raising

- Review your social media profiles, especially LinkedIn and make sure they align with what you want people to think about you
- Broaden your network – LinkedIn is great for this and people are very open to receiving connections
- Get out there – make the effort to attend sector events and funder events and read about trends and developments in your field
- Become a thought leader – if you've got opinions on how things could be done differently or are passionate about a particular subject

# KNOW YOURSELF

In order to be as good as you can be at your job, you need to have an accurate understanding of your strengths, weaknesses and personality traits.

**Why self-awareness is important in leadership**
If you know what your strengths are then you can choose roles that play to those strengths, develop them further and sell yourself effectively at interviews. If you know your weaknesses then you can improve upon them and be careful not to select jobs that depend upon them. The more you know about yourself, the stronger the position you will be in.

When we think of strengths and weaknesses we often think about natural aptitudes (or lack thereof) such as numeracy, confidence, punctuality etc. but it is helpful to think more widely than that. They could also be around gaps in your knowledge or experience, how you work under pressure, what you bring to a meeting or how you treat other people. Your strengths can also include the things that you are passionate about and the energy you bring to a situation.

As a leader your strengths and weaknesses are magnified because people are looking to you for leadership, guidance and decisions. For example, if you are disorganised and last minute about everything, that is going to be hard for people who work for you. You'll be making them work late on pitches or documents, which could cause frustration, and if you're late or consistently cancel their 1:1 meetings with you then they will feel unvalued. Conversely if, for example, you are positive, even in times of disappointment then that sets the tone for others to follow and impacts upon the general energy and resilience of your team.

**Gathering information about yourself**
Many of us have a distorted view of ourselves, based on feedback we've received from people along the way and our own assumptions. Very often feedback is context specific and can often say more about the person giving

the feedback than the person receiving it – so how do we uncover an accurate assessment of ourselves?

- **Personality profiles** – undertaking a widely-used personality profile assessment can give you some very valuable information about yourself and help you to understand more about you. Myers-Briggs is widely used, as is Insights. Both give you information on a number of different aspects of your personality and they provide a shared language for understanding tensions within and between teams.
- **Strengths Finder 2.0** – this is a book and online test by Tom Rath that profiles 34 different strengths and helps you to identify your combination of strengths. It also gives tailored advice on how to develop yourself based on your particular profile.
- **360 degree feedback** – consider requesting a 360 degree appraisal even if it is not widely used in your organisation. You have to have a thick skin but it can tell you what your team think of you and highlight how you are both helping them and potentially holding them back. You could also create your own 360 degree survey and ask people in your team what they feel your strengths and weaknesses as a leader are or use staff surveys to gather feedback anonymously about the management team.
- **Skills and knowledge audit** – review job descriptions and person specifications for roles like yours and those you want to apply for in the future and map your skills, knowledge and experience against them.
- **Coaching** – an executive coach can help you to uncover for yourself the areas where you excel and the areas you are struggling with. They can also help you to reflect on the best way to develop yourself – it is essentially training that is completely tailored to you and gives you tools you can use at work on a daily basis.
- **Find a mentor** – a mentor can help you to see your strengths and weaknesses in a broader context within the sector and can inspire you to develop new skills and knowledge.
- **Map your successes** and what they had in common and you will find the magic that you bring to a situation.

## Should you be an all-rounder or focus on your strengths?
None of us likes having weaknesses but should we be trying to be good at everything or should we focus our attention on playing to our strengths? There are different schools of thought on this topic.

On the one hand, it isn't good to have glaring gaps in your knowledge, skills and experience as a leader. You may not have hands-on experience of certain income streams for example but you can always talk to peers, go on courses and read until you know the key things to look for and the main success factors. Equally it isn't really acceptable to claim that you're stuck with your more annoying habits such as being late or losing your temper. You are a professional and there are certain minimum standards that we all have to conform to, whether it comes naturally or takes huge effort.

But is being an all-rounder who is good at everything always the best option? If you are by nature an all-rounder then embrace that – it is a strength in itself. But many of us have more pronounced strengths and weaknesses and can only truly excel when we can build on and play to our strengths. There is an approach to career management called the Strengths Movement which says you should focus your work life on the things you're good at, and steer yourself away from the things you're bad at.

As leading career management thought leader Marcus Buckingham says, *"You have development needs — areas where you need to grow, areas where you need to get better — but for you, as for all of us, you will learn the most, grow the most, and develop the most in your areas of greatest strength. Your strengths are your multiplier. Your strengths magnify you."*

The most successful fundraising leaders fall into two camps. Some are genuinely great all-rounders and others know what they excel at and make sure that their role focuses on that. They also build a team around them that balances and challenges them. Often the secret to success is picking the organisation whose needs and culture really needs someone with your strengths.

### Knowing what you need from your manager

The other benefit of knowing yourself is that you can be clear with your manager what you need from them in order to be able to perform well. Best communicated at interview rather than after a year in post, it can be really helpful to share with your manager how to get the best out of you. Whether it's praise, recognition, attention, freedom, autonomy, financial reward or status, if you understand what really motivates you then you are a step ahead of most people. And if your manager can't provide that then get creative with other ways to get what you need.

Kath Abrahams of Diabetes UK on knowing yourself and leadership…

*"My first thought on that is there is no single blueprint for being a leader. I think the most important thing is to be who you are. To be comfortable in your own skin, with all the shortcomings that that involves. To be comfortable in that space of thinking "I bring some things. I don't bring everything. Sometimes that will be the right thing for an organisation. Sometimes it won't be the right thing. That's fine". I think that level of comfort enables me to be comfortable in a role that is full of ambiguity, and that has good days and bad days. That is full of successes and failures. To be able to say, this is the way that I'm going to lead people through that. That's the best I can do."*

**Further reading & resources**
You can find out more about your strengths using Strengths Finder 2.0 by Tom Rath and more about why to focus on your strengths by reading Go Put Your Strengths To Work by Marcus Buckingham

Personality profiles - Myers-Briggs and Insights are both widely used.

# INVESTING IN YOURSELF

If you've read the previous chapter, Know Yourself, then you will be starting from the strong place of understanding what areas of your skills, knowledge, experience and attributes you would like to develop.

**Think long-term & set career goals**
Hopefully you are going to have a career in the charity sector for a long time, so it is worth spending some time considering what you want to achieve career-wise and what roles you might like to have in the future. If you love managing and leading then you might want to consider a long term goal to be a Fundraising Director (if you're currently heading up an income stream) or a Chief Executive. If you love fundraising but have no interest in moving up the ladder perhaps you want to work for, or create, the best corporate/individual giving/community team in the sector.

If you are not sure how you want to develop your career then you might want to try meeting with a career coach who can help you to work out what would be the best career route for you.

Not everyone naturally sets themselves career goals but if you find yourself frustrated at the slow progress of your career it can be helpful to create some career goals. Once I started leading teams and working on strategies I realised that being a Fundraising Director would suit me and challenge me - so I set myself a goal to be a Fundraising Director by the time I was 30. I made choices that helped me to reach that goal, many of which you'll find in the chapter on preparing to step up. I reached that goal aged 29 and when I realised 5 years later that being a CEO would allow me to create change more effectively I set myself that long-term goal too. I've since been Interim CEO of a small charity and Managing Director of a business.

I realised that my key driver is around creating change, and in particular organisational change and so for me it made sense to aim for a position that gave me the ultimate ability to do that. Your passion might be around major donors or the ability to work internationally or around a particular cause that you would love to raise funds for. Whatever it is write it down, imagine it happening and keep your radar on for opportunities that could help you to get closer to achieving your goal.

**What does excellent look like?**

When I coach leaders looking to improve their performance and effectiveness, I always ask them "what would excellent look like in your role?" Often people haven't thought about that and there is a useful coaching tool that you can use to structure your thinking about this.

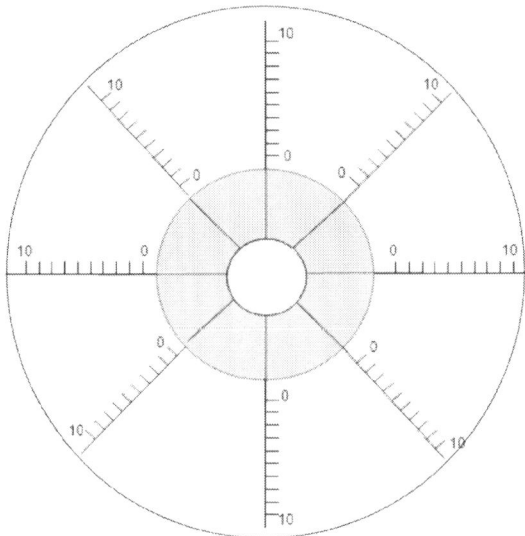

This is a coaching wheel. It is split into 8 sections.

1. Make a list of 8 elements of your role that you think you need to be excellent at e.g. budgeting, managing direct reports, major donor cultivation.
2. Write down a description of what excellence would look like for each element.
3. Assign each element a segment of your wheel by writing them around the outside of the wheel.
4. Rate your current performance for each element on a scale of 1 to 10
5. Make a mark on each segment to reflect your rating of 1 to 10
6. Identify which areas are most in need of attention i.e. those with the lowest ratings
7. For each of those areas work out what action would take you one

point higher up the scale. For example, if you gave yourself 5 out of 10 for finance you could arrange a meeting with your finance director to go through some basics and increase your understanding to reach 6 out of 10?
8. Make an action plan for the improvements you want to make. Remember that you are not aiming to go straight to a 10 out of 10 in every area. Effective change has to be realistic and manageable.
9. Check in on your progress each month and set new tasks to move a step closer to 10 out of 10. In 6 months you could be excellent at everything!

## Developing yourself

Here are some ideas on how to develop yourself as a leader. Your employer may be happy to invest in your training and development - it is always worth asking and making the business case for that investment.

- **Coaching** – working with a coach can help you break through the mental barriers that are standing in your way, keep you energised and focused and become more resilient. I found coaching really helpful when I first became a Director as I could speak honestly about the challenges I was facing and develop my confidence.
- **Mentoring** – mentors can be hugely valuable. Traditionally a mentor commits to supporting you for a period of time and meets you regularly. However successful people are often busy so I have always found it easier to find a group of individuals that I can have coffee with every now and then and contact when I need advice on a particular topic. For me this is around projects that I want to launch and specialist expertise I'd like access to as well as the inspiration I get from the energy of those people. And I am not formally a mentor to anyone but I am often contacted by people who have worked for me in the past to talk through their next move or a job offer and I'm delighted to be able to help them.
- **Qualifications** – you can study fundraising and charity leadership at a number of universities including Cass Business School and London South Bank University. The Institute of Fundraising offers both a Diploma and a Masters level International Advanced Diploma. You might also consider an MBA and whilst they are very expensive, there are often scholarships available for people from the sector. Another interesting option is the Clore Social Leadership Programme for people looking to have a large impact on the sector.
- **Training** – as well as the Institute of Fundraising and Directory of Social Change there are lots of training providers that run open

programmes including major donor specialists such as Rob Wood and Solid Management. If you're looking to become more efficient and productive then check out Think Productive. Those are just the trainers that I know personally but there are lots of others out there across the country.
- **Trusteeship** – as mentioned in previous chapters, becoming a Trustee can be a great way to learn about running charities.

Jenni Anderson of Haven House on how she has developed herself…

*"I would consider myself a professional fundraiser. By that, I mean, I've spent time educating myself and I've been lucky to have learnt from others inside and outside of the organisations I've worked in. If you just look inwardly, you're never going to develop.*

*I completed the MSc charities pathway at Cass Business School. I found that hugely beneficial. It's an MBA for the charity sector. It goes through all of the things that charities need to do to be sustainable. Governance, resources, HR, the whole gamut. It's a safe learning environment, where it's okay to ask stupid questions, it's okay to have debates, it's okay to be challenged back as well. I would recommend that."*

# YOUR LEADERSHIP STYLE

The way that you lead your team has a big impact on the team. Research by Daniel Goleman published in Harvard Business Review showed that leadership style of senior staff is responsible for 30% of the company's bottom line profitability.

You probably have a leadership style that comes naturally to you, but it can be really helpful to be able to flex your leadership style to meet the needs of the situation you are facing. The best leaders are able to adapt their approach in order to help their team perform effectively.

I'd like to share with you an increasingly popular leadership style called Transformational Leadership. This style aligns closely with the suggestions that I have been sharing in this book and the way that the Fundraising Directors interviewed in the book talk about their approach to leadership.

### Transformational Leadership

Initially described by James McGregor Burns as a process "where leaders and their followers raise one another to higher levels of morality and motivation" this concept was then further developed by Bernard M Bass in his book "Leadership and Performance Beyond Expectations".

A transformational leader…
- Is a model of integrity and fairness
- Sets clear goals
- Has high expectations
- Encourages others
- Provides support and recognition
- Stirs the emotions of people
- Gets people to look beyond their self-interest
- Inspires people to reach for the improbable

The way that transformational leaders do this is to create an inspiring vision of the future, motivate people to take ownership of and deliver the vision, make that vision happen and build strong and trust-based relationships. You will find lots of information and ideas to help you do that in the other chapters of this book.

**Path-Goal Theory**
Transformational leadership works well as a whole team approach but there will be times when you are line-managing people with diverse experience who will need different things from you as a line manager. Highly experienced team members and inexperienced team members will require very different approaches, as will high performing individuals and poor performing individuals. Path-Goal theory articulates which management approaches to use in those situations.

The theory assumes that the role of a manager is to help their direct reports to identify goals which align with organisational goals, help them to achieve those goals and help tackle any obstacles to achieving those goals. These are the 4 approaches you can take…

- **Directive & clarifying** – you are very clear about what is expected of the individual and how you want them to perform their tasks. It is best used when a task or project is inherently ambiguous or when the individual is inexperienced or performing poorly.
- **Achievement-orientated** – you set challenging goals, expect the individual to perform at their highest level and have confidence in them to achieve those goals. This approach is best used with experienced senior staff.
- **Participative** – you collaborate and consult on decisions so that the individual has genuine input. This approach is best used with senior staff on complex projects.
- **Supportive** – this is aimed at supporting the individual and being sensitive to their needs and is best used when tasks are stressful.

**Six Emotional Leadership Styles**
In their book "Primal Leadership" Daniel Goleman, Richard Boyatzis and Annie McKee outlined 6 leadership styles and their emotional impact on teams. You'll see that you can draw on whichever style you need in order to deal with the situation you face. I've summarised them here but I recommend reading the book.

- **The Visionary leader** – sets out the vision and motivates people

to achieve it. They are empathetic and explain how and why people's efforts contribute to the vision. This approach brings people together and it works well when a new direction is needed and has a positive emotional impact in the team.
- **The Coaching leader** – listens, helps people identify their strengths and weaknesses, encourages and delegates. This approach connects what an individual wants with the goals of the organisation. It has a positive emotional impact on the team and is useful for helping competent and motivated people to improve performance by building long-term capabilities.
- **The Affiliative leader** – puts people first and creates an emotional bond between them and the organisation. They promote harmony, boost morale and resolve conflicts. The team feel more connected to each other so it is a good style to use when there has been a breakdown of trust or to motivate people in stressful times. It should not be used exclusively though as it can be hard to use it to get high performance or set direction.
- **The Democratic leader** – builds consensus through participation and asks people what they think. The team feel valued and commit by participating. It can be useful when you need your team to take ownership of a decision or project or when your team know more than you do (I found this really useful when I ran a recruitment company of experienced recruiters when I was new to the sector). This approach doesn't work well in times of crisis, if a quick decision is needed or if the team feel they don't know enough.
- **The Pacesetting leader** – expects and models excellence with a strong drive to achieve. Leads by example but can lack empathy. This can work well when a team is motivated and experienced and the leader needs quick results. Used in other situations it can be overwhelming and demotivating for team members.
- **The Coercive leader** – demands immediate compliance "do as I tell you". Good in a crisis or as a last resort with a poor performing team member but should otherwise be avoided because it alienates people and create an unhappy team.

## Communicating with your team

On my travels in the sector I have often heard people say that they have no idea what their Fundraising Director or CEO were doing with their time, with the implication being that the people at the top don't work as hard as everyone else. It is important that your team understands your role and the value you add to the organisation and the best way to ensure that is to communicate with them. I ask my teams to create a monthly report on their activities, plans and achievements and I also contribute a section myself (as well as editing it). That allows me to tell them about the meetings I've been to, the influencing I've been doing and my main projects and priorities. I also sit with the team so that they see me working hard. I'm confident that those two communication tools mean no one who has worked in my teams has ever questioned what I'm doing with my time.

Have regular 1:1s with your team members, even if you sit next to them and they are highly experienced. It shows that they are a priority to you (so don't frequently cancel or move them), it gives them a place where they can raise any issues and it will be invaluable if they later start performing poorly.

Jools Tait of BEN on her management style…

*"It isn't all my way or the highway. It isn't all about the director's ego, it is about positive motivation. It's give praise and credit, where credit is due, it's passing it down. Building that sense of team and talking the "I" out of it for want of a better expression. Succession planning is key and keeping people and building their skills and experience, I think you hold onto your workforce for longer.*

*But it's also taking the time to inspire and lead your team with your aspirations and your vision for the team. And also I think when you are in a more senior role, it's important not to forget that you are also part of that team. I think it is a combination of how you set the culture of the team and that mutual respect, people having a voice, being able to listen. It's bringing them with you on the journey."*

Mark Astarita of British Red Cross on his management style…

*"Personally I am an open book emotionally. I give of myself, am very loyal to my people and trust massively. I have in the last 25 years rarely been disappointed. I think I only do one thing really well and that is find great people to work with. Makes work great and rarely a chore."*

**Further reading…**
"Primal Leadership" by Daniel Goleman, Richard Boyatzis and Annie McKee

# RESILIENCE

Leading a fundraising team can be tough. There's a lot of pressure to reach and even exceed your targets. There's always more work that could be done and sometimes your hard work doesn't turn into the results you'd like. And that's assuming all your team are happy and performing well. Whilst all that is going on, you have to lead your team through the ups and downs with optimism and positivity.

The more resilient you are, the easier it will be to keep yourself and your team positive in tough times.

**Managing your energy**
It takes physical, mental and emotional energy to be an inspiring team leader who is on top of everything. And your energy is a limited resource. If you keep expending more energy than you have then you'll end up feeling exhausted and demotivated and may even get sick. This is known as burnout and is surprisingly common among senior fundraisers.

The secret to being able to keep your energy levels high is to find ways to top up your energy and commit to making them part of your daily and weekly routine. Make sure you're doing some physical exercise and find out what works for you when it comes to stress relief and recharging your batteries. It might be going for a run, taking a yoga class, or if things are really bad, punching your frustrations out at a boxing class.

It's also important to eat well and not fuel yourself with the constant supply of sweets and cake that seem to be present in most fundraising teams. Make sugar a treat or you'll end up relying on it to get past 4pm every day. Why not pack healthy snacks or have an office fruit bowl instead?

Find some things to do that make you feel like "you". Whether you love to draw, dance, hang out with your kids or write poems, you will feel happier and more grounded if you prioritise making time for yourself.

I also suggest making a list of things that make you happy or that you'd like to try and scheduling them into your diary so that whatever is going on at work you always have something to look forward to.

**Setting boundaries**
Be clear with yourself on what hours you're going to work as standard and how often you'll go beyond that. Your job is endless and you could be there all night, every night if you don't set some limits. It can be hard when your CEO is sending you midnight emails but lead by example and focus on getting your job done well in working hours rather than constantly burning the midnight oil. And don't send emails and texts to your team out of office hours unless you truly need to – it makes everyone feel like they are constantly on call and should be working.

**Managing your emotions**
Believe it or not, it is possible to care too much about your job. If you emotionally over-invest in your job then it becomes more than a job, it becomes part of who you are. Which motivates you to work harder but when it's not going well then it can feel like your whole life isn't going well. And if your job come under criticism it becomes difficult not to take it personally.

Placing too much of your self-worth in your job can mean you lose perspective and perspective is a very useful skill for a team leader to have. You need to lead without being swayed by your own emotions and you can only do that if you are able to take a step back and see what's actually going on.

Fundraisers, being great relationship builders, are often quite intuitive and make decisions based on their gut instinct and experience. And there is definitely a place for that but you also have to be able to look at decisions from another perspective, particularly when you're managing income streams that are new to you. Make sure that you are gathering all the relevant information, actively seeking opinions which are different from yours and taking an analytical approach if that doesn't come naturally to you. You'll benefit from that and so will those that work with you.

**Mindfulness & perspective**
Mindfulness, or meditation which is at the heart of mindfulness, is becoming increasingly popular in business as well as for individuals. Scientific studies show that regular meditators experience less stress, more creativity, are better at focusing and staying on tasks and communicate better during conflict. That's a lot of benefits for spending 10 minutes a day just sitting and breathing.

It's particularly helpful if you lead a team because it creates perspective. If you have trained your mind to recognise that your thoughts and emotions come and go, then you are less controlled by those thoughts and emotions. Most of us, if we were wronged, would dwell on it, get angry about it, second-guess how we dealt with it and carry it with us for the rest of the day. Regular meditators have trained their mind to notice "I'm angry" or "I can't stop thinking about what happened", which removes them from some of the strength of those thoughts and emotions and they've also trained themselves to drop unhelpful thoughts and emotions. So they can feel it, let it go and stop revisiting it.

There are non-religious apps like Headspace which train you to meditate or you can find your own way of gaining a bit of space and perspective when you recognise your emotions are running high. Perhaps go and get some fresh air or look at photos that make you smile or think about the cause you're working to support.

**Getting support**

If things feel too much, make sure you get some support. It is a sign of strength to say that you are struggling, not a sign of weakness. Some organisations offer employee helplines, if not then have a chat to your HR manager or line manager. Getting a coach can also help you prioritise, manage your time more effectively and offer a confidential place to discuss your challenges.

# PRODUCTIVITY AND PRIORITISING

**What are your real priorities?**
There's a difference between your to do list and your priorities. Your to do list has a lot of tasks on it and your diary is full of meetings and so those things tend to take priority. But what about spending time with your team informally getting to know them and seeing how they're doing? What about taking time to be creative or to read about the latest developments in fundraising? Do those things ever even make it onto your to do list? And, if not, how often do you make time for them?

A good way to start is to set aside some time to think about what you are trying to achieve this year as an individual. What would make this a great year for you professionally? What do you need to do to be more effective in your role? What things are important to you but never get to the top of your to do list? That way you get to decide your priorities rather than other people deciding them for you by assigning you tasks or putting meetings in your diary.

Kate Collins of Teenage Cancer Trust on what she has learnt about prioritising...

*"Since I became a director, one of my learnings has been to understand what makes me productive in a different way. I've realised that actually being good at my job isn't about strategies and budgets. Those are important, but those are almost the hygiene factors, it's kind of a given you can do those. It's all the other stuff, the soft stuff.*

*Because when you need to have a difficult conversation or something comes up that's a challenge within or for the organisation, that's when you need to have the bank of goodwill and trust and connection. And if you haven't invested the time in people to have goodwill in the bank, you could be technically brilliant but if you're on your own, it's pretty bloody lonely, and it doesn't work.*

*I used to spend almost all my time in the office in pre-arranged back-to-back meetings. By contrast, today I've had loads of meetings, but many of those have been informal, unplanned conversations that have needed to happen.*

*And planning for informal interaction has become really important. I now give myself time in the morning to chat to people and I believe that a lot of my job is about relationships, connections and talking. If I look at my diary and think 'I've only got one meeting, is it worth going to London?' that's probably the day I most need to be in London because I'll get such richness of connection and conversation. What I shouldn't do is try to write documents on those days, because there's no point coming to London and sitting behind a closed office door.*

*Lots of people I work with also work from home or are on the move a lot, so I try and to use my at home time to do calls and get my head down writing reports."*

## Productivity tools and technology

When you have decided on your priorities then I recommend using systems to organise yourself as much as possible. If you have a system in place then it creates habits and habits are the most efficient way to tackle regular tasks. You don't waste minutes each morning and evening deliberating over whether it is the right time to brush your teeth do you? No, you just do it without thinking and can usually think about something else for those 2 minutes as well. The other reason to have systems in place is a theory called "ego depletion" which claims that we all have a limited supply of willpower, and it decreases with overuse. If you have systems in place that you don't question then you're not using up any willpower.

I read a fascinating article in Vanity Fair, which followed Barack Obama around for 6 months. Obama has routinized the everyday elements of his life as much as possible and this is why…

*"You'll see I wear only grey or blue suits. I'm trying to pare down decisions. I don't want to make decisions about what I'm eating or wearing. Because I have too many other decisions to make… you need to focus your decision-making energy. You need to routinize yourself. You can't be going through the day distracted by trivia."*

Here are some suggestions of simple but useful systems to help keep you organised…

- Always **confirm external meetings** a day or two before and make sure you know where you're going and how to get there (I started doing that after too many meetings that were a no show and too many stressed out running late moments trying to find the address on my phone)
- **Schedule travel time** into your calendar

- Write **tomorrow's to do list** at the end of each day
- Identify which tasks will have the **greatest impact** and start with those
- Have a system for **checking and organising your inbox.** There are also apps such as mailbox where you can schedule emails to come back into your inbox at a relevant point, which works well with tickets for events.
- Have a physical or virtual **to do list** – I love a notebook but there are some great apps like Wanderlist and todoist
- If you find yourself running out of time it can be helpful to **track your time** for a week so that you can see where it is going and identify where it is being wasted
- Cut down on **non-essential email** but making it policy not to cc anyone unless it is absolutely necessary and then come up with a more efficient way of sharing key information such as a monthly report
- Focus on the task at hand and **avoid distractions** as it takes time to switch between tasks and be productive again. If you're working on something important turn off your email alerts, put your smartphone in a drawer and turn off your web browser. You'll notice if you're addicted to incoming information if you're twitching to press buttons when you do that.

It's worth asking the most efficient and successful people you know how they organise their work and life as they'll no doubt have some great systems and tactics to keep them on track.

You should also consider what sort of example you are setting your team. It's hard to hold someone accountable for missing a deadline if you're missing deadlines. Your actions must align with what you're saying and you need to set higher standards for yourself than you set for your team. That is only going to be possible if you set some boundaries and don't say yes to everything and if you learn how to delegate well.

**Further reading...**
"How to be a Productivity Ninja" by Graham Allcott, a former charity CEO

# DELEGATION

*"No person will make a great business who wants to do it all himself or get all the credit."*
Andrew Carnegie

There are many benefits to getting great at delegating. It will save you time. It ensures that the resources of the charity are allocated in a cost-effective way because you won't be being paid a senior salary to carry out tasks that could be done by one of your team. It also gives others an opportunity to learn and develop themselves and it can help to train your successor. If you delegate well then you give your direct reports the permission to do the same and the whole team becomes more efficient.

**Delegation can be tricky**
People often find delegation hard to get right. These are the things that often go wrong…

- Some people don't like asking others to do "their work" and feel it is imposing
- Others think "I can do this quicker myself"
- It can be hard to let go of 'control' and pass work to others
- You want it done 'right' (i.e. your way) and then you are disappointed when it is approached differently
- The briefing and handover of the task are rushed or poorly executed
- People delegate the tasks they just don't want to do or have run out of time for
- The task is not at the right skill level for the person you are giving it to
- The project really needs your input or that of someone more senior than you
- You don't ask someone to carry out a task - you tell them and without advance warning

**Getting it right**
Here are some key parts of the process of effective delegation…
- **Do you need to delegate?** Are you struggling to get through your to do list? Stressed and working long hours? Lacking the time to focus on strategy and important donor relationships? Those are all signs that you would benefit from delegating. Also look at whether you are missing opportunities to develop your direct reports by not delegating meetings and events to them if you are unable to attend.
- **Identify projects that could be delegated.** Not everything will be a good project to delegate. It should be a distinct project in itself rather than part of a larger process. It cannot be dependent on your constant input or that of people more senior than you. It should be time-measured so that it can be realistically built into workloads. It needs to be clearly defined.
- **Identify the right person to delegate to.** Do they have the skills, knowledge and experience to deliver on this project? Do they have the time? Will they need any training or to attend any key meetings before they take on the task? Are they keen to take on more work? Will they approach it with the level of detail or creative thinking that you have in mind? Are there any internal political issues with your choice?
- **Give them advance warning**. Make sure that you are not dumping a task on someone last minute. And ask them nicely with a brief explanation of the task and why you chose them to delegate it to.
- **Brief them on the task**. This should include…
    - Context of the task/project
    - Why you selected them and what you think they bring to the project
    - In-depth description of the task and process
    - Key outputs and outcomes
    - Resources available to them
    - Support you will offer
    - Decision-making remit – are there decisions you want to be consulted on?
    - The updates you would like – frequency and level of detail
    - Whether or not you want to be copied in on relevant emails
    - How you would like them to approach the task (if necessary or a junior staff member)
    - Timings and deadlines

## Following up

- **Be available.** Make sure that you are available to your colleague if they need you and check in – but not too often! They may well have clarifying questions to ask you once they get started on the project.
- **Manage the messaging.** If there is any chance that delegating this project could cause internal issues (which may happen if it is seen as a development opportunity) then think carefully about how you proactively manage the communication of the project delegation to the team.
- **Give credit.** It is really important that you give credit to the person doing all the work.
- **Feedback.** Take the time to give feedback on the project.
- **Say thank you**

One final point on delegation. If you are delegating to an experienced manager or head of team, you need to have the trust in them to let them run the project their way. They are good at their job and got that way by working in a way that works for them. If you ask them to essentially become a clone of you and do it all exactly how you would do it, then they will get frustrated and you will be disappointed. If you are delegating responsibility for the project then respect their way of approaching it.

*"Don't tell people how to do things, tell them what to do and let them surprise you with their results."*
George S. Patton, wartime US General

Kath Abrahams of Diabetes UK on delegating...

*"Part of what I'm trying to bring here is a sense of empowering people as I firmly believe people are able to step up and take responsibility. That's what they want to do, and I know from my own personal experience, that I've performed best when I've worked for people who trusted me, rather than people who've controlled and questioned and limited what I'm able to do."*

# GROWTH MINDSET

**What is a growth mindset?**
Your mindset determines your beliefs about yourself, your life and the world. It is the lens through which you process life's events and it influences your actions and therefore the results you get. Research by Dr Carol Dweck, a Stanford psychologist, identified that there are two types of mindset – a fixed mindset and a growth mindset.

A "fixed" mindset assumes that character, intelligence, and creative ability are set in stone and determine how successful we are in life. Someone with a fixed mindset often sees failure as a sign that they'll never be good at something and can avoid challenges in order to feel successful.

A "growth" mindset assumes that character, intelligence and creative ability can be developed and that hard work and learning from failure will determine how successful we are in life. Someone with a growth mindset sees failure as feedback, is more resilient and seeks out challenges.

Many successful entrepreneurs, such as Richard Branson, have a growth mindset, which has allowed them to bounce back from failure and take more risks.

*"Ultimately I think that people must learn from the times that things don't work out for them. Those can be the best lessons of your life."*
Richard Branson

*"We all have some wins, we all have some losses. It's a clichéd point, but the trick is to celebrate the wins and learn from the losses. The thing about failure is that it's temporary and imagined, it's not really real, it's what you choose to tell yourself in your head. The great thing is you can choose to tell yourself something different. Tell yourself, 'Okay, that didn't work out, why not? Now I understand, bank that learning and move on.'"*
Richard Reed, co-founder at Innocent

We all err towards one of these mindsets, although there may be areas of our lives that have different mindsets. For example, at work I have a growth mindset – I value challenges, I don't take failure personally and I want to constantly learn. However if you try and teach me to ski you'll find I have a fixed mindset – I'm terrified and think I'll never be any good at it because my first few attempts went badly and were no fun. The good news is that once you are aware of your mindset you can take steps to consciously develop a growth mindset.

## Mindset & leadership

Have a think about which mindset you err towards at work. Do you feel like your career is full of potential and is what you make it or do you feel stuck? Do you find failure hard to accept and bounce back from? Are you convinced that there are some things you're just not good at or is the world your oyster?

If you have a fixed mindset about work or some areas of work, why not commit to develop more of a growth mindset? You'll find the book recommended later really helpful for that.

## Embedding growth mindset for your team

As a team leader it's really helpful to have a growth mindset. You'll be more open to innovation, more resilient and can lead by positive example. A leader with a growth mindset sees the potential in their team. Rather than seeing ability as fixed, they take a coaching approach to developing their team.

Imagine if all of your team were constantly improving, learning and developing themselves and their knowledge. If they could take setbacks in their stride (so important for fundraisers) and could always see the potential in a situation. You would never hear "we tried that and it didn't work".

Here are some ways to embed a growth mindset in your team…

- Evaluate key activities regularly, making it clear that things which went "wrong" provide valuable information
- Encourage the team to look for ways to incrementally improve the way you deal with donors
- Embrace tough times as part of the journey towards success
- Make it okay to fail. It's one thing to say it, another to not look disappointed when a new fundraising idea gets a poor response.
- Lead by example and admit your own struggles and failures, past and present

- Praise people for effort as well as achievement

Jenni Anderson of Haven House on growth mindset...

*"Everyone has bad days, and things that don't pay off. You predominantly have to have a positive outlook on life, which then means that when you have setbacks and you do muck up and make mistakes, yourself as well as your team, you are not going to let that cloud everything else that you do."*

**Further reading**
"Mindset" by Dr Carol Dweck and also her TED talk

# MANAGING YOUR TEAM

# CREATING YOUR TEAM'S CULTURE

*"Culture is simply a shared way of doing something with a passion"*
Brian Chesky, Co-founder of AirBnB

A strong and positive culture is at the heart of all successful fundraising teams but there is no single 'ideal' culture. I've seen great teams that were highly structured and also great teams which were much more fluid and flexible. I've seen great teams that felt incredibly commercial with super high standards of professionalism as a priority and equally great teams that prioritised enjoyable interactions with each other and supporters above all else.

You need to create a culture that works for your team, your organisation and also, to some extent, your leadership style. If your organisation already has a clearly defined culture it is important that your team aligns with that. I suggest sticking to the organisational values and focusing most on those that make most sense for fundraising. The same principle applies if you're running a team within the wider fundraising team.

*"There's no magic formula for great company culture. The key is just to treat your staff how you would like to be treated."*
Richard Branson

**So how do you create a team culture?**
The simple answer to that is – as a team. Changing a culture is a big endeavour. Even if you have been hired to turn around a dysfunctional team or you have a clear picture in your head of what you want to create, you need to take everybody with you on that journey or it will be impossible to embed your new culture.

The best way to discuss team culture is to take some time together out of the office on an away day. I facilitate a lot of these away days and here some ideas for that process which you can adapt to fit your team…

- **Relationship building icebreaker** – I often have a race to see who can find as many different things in common with their colleagues as possible (excluding the more obvious answers) and it's great to see people discover they both love baking or horses or grew up in the same town. The point is to remind people what they have in common.
- Set some ground rules around creating a safe space and avoiding blaming people and personal comments. Then ask people to **describe your team culture as it is now** – the good, the bad and the ambiguous. One safe way to do this is to describe the high features of a successful fundraising team and ask people to rate where they think the team is currently for each of those features and then overall. You can do that physically by creating a scale with numbers on the floor, which gets everyone moving around.
- Get the team thinking about **what would be a great culture to work in**. If you want to make sure everyone contributes ask them to spend some time writing their ideas on post it notes and then they can come up and share them.
- Building on the post it notes, brainstorm collectively around what would be a great culture to work in. Questions to ask yourselves could include…
    - How will supporters feel after coming into contact with us?
    - How will our colleagues describe us?
    - How will we deal with each other when we are under pressure or feeling tired?
    - How will we tackle tensions between teams?
    - How will we celebrate success?
    - How will we learn from failure?
    - How will we know if we've become more efficient? And effective?
- **Agree your top 10** list of what you want your culture to look like and then add in how you will know you have succeeded.
- Think about a creative way to **represent this visually** so that you can all have a reminder of your culture
- **Everyone commits** to playing an active role is creating and embedding this culture
- Agree how you will **track and celebrate** your progress

Got a shy or reluctant crowd? A bit of friendly competition and plenty of bags of Percy Pigs for the winners gets target-driven fundraisers involved in your various challenges, ice breakers etc. One my clients asked team members to take turns to run short ice breakers between sessions on a two day strategy day and it was great to see the creative games they came up with.

Mark Astarita of British Red Cross on culture…

*"Celebrate success. I know it's a very egalitarian sector. People say "Oh I don't know if I want to celebrate anyone over and above everyone else, everyone's contribution is important." I think we thrive on a bit of a pat on the back. As a workforce, I think, we're clearly not motivated by personal gain otherwise we wouldn't be working in the sector. That doesn't mean we don't love it when people applaud us for what we do and give us a pat on the back. Small amounts of effort going into that can be hugely valuable."*

Kate Collins of Teenage Cancer Trust on team culture…

*"For me the key challenge right now is all about keeping our fabulous culture as we grow. Yes, you know you've got to make sure the money comes in at the right return. But the team are really good at that. The team don't need me to worry about that. If they need me to worry, I know they will tell me to worry and when they need me to help me with that, they will pull me in to work with them.*

*It is about not losing some of the intangible cultural elements of the organisation, the ones that actually meant that when we didn't have a complex formal strategy we were still doing a great job. And actually playing and laughing is really important at Teenage Cancer Trust. We are a young organisation, we look after young people. And I would very much hope that we are raising money through relationships in a way that fits with the organisation."*

Kath Abrahams of Diabetes UK on culture…

*"I'm quite a gut feel, instinctive person. I get a sense of culture by talking to people. By hearing the words they use. I like environments where people talk to each other and work together as a matter of course. When I first started at Breakthrough, I noticed people who sat next to each other and opposite to each other were emailing each other sometimes. That's the stuff that I try and change. Some of that's about the way I try and behave. I try and do as much as possible going and talking to people. Very deliberately and I make sure that I hear about the work people have done so that I can talk to them about it. Other people see that I'm doing that. Some of it's about the signals that you send."*

# CROSS-TEAM WORKING

Getting teams to work effectively together is a universal problem within organisations and one that often comes up when I'm coaching leaders. If fundraising is about great relationship building then that needs to start internally – within your team and between teams in your organisation. Ultimately creating a culture where people consider themselves first and foremost as part of the fundraising team comes down to creating a strong sense of what it means to be part of the fundraising team. If you have taken the time to define and create the culture of your team then you are already a step closer.

In fundraising teams that haven't got this right you often see disputes between teams over where income sits and tension about resources. You also see little sharing of information as everyone focuses on their income stream and feels a sense of ownership over 'their' donors. As a result nobody is looking at fundraising from the perspective of the donor themselves who has no idea what 'team' they sit in and just wants to be valued as a person and donor. Quite often people in these fundraising teams don't build strong friendships outside of their income stream and sometimes they are actively negative about some of their colleagues.

In teams that have effective cross-team working there is a sense that you are all on the same team and working towards the same common goal. They have a process in place for dealing with income that could sit in a number of income lines and everyone delights in the success of their colleagues. They try and think from the donor's perspective and are not placing the boundaries or jargon of the organisation ahead of building a strong relationship with donors. They like each other, flaws and all, and choose to spend time together socially sometimes. Speaking negatively about another colleague or team is not part of the culture and is quickly shut down if it happens.

## Your role as leader

Once you have worked with your team on culture it is the role of you and your heads of team to embed that culture. There are a few elements to this, which are simple but often forgotten…

- **Model good behaviour** and show your team how you want things to be done. You can't expect your team to not fight about income if they see you taking a similar attitude on any areas where you have tension with your fellow Directors. Equally if you are not treating the whole organisation as 'one team' and are setting the fundraising team apart, then you are not modelling a team approach. Make sure that you are giving credit to colleagues in other departments and are not speaking negatively about any of your colleagues.
- **Reward good behaviour and provide structures that support it.** Draw attention to teams working well together on projects and events during your team meetings and in your reports. Share examples of how donor relationships were improved by thinking of a donor as a person who could give via their company, foundation or personally rather than as a 'major donor' or 'trust'. Consider putting relationship fundraising at the heart of your structure. You could also create a soft credits system to reflect money raised thanks to the support of another department – this is often used for corporate runners using community fundraising marathon places for example. If there are queries over where income sits, be clear on the rationale you use for decision-making and be consistent, creating a clear process where possible.
- **Set clear boundaries.** Don't ignore behaviour that goes against the principles you've set around culture and cross-team working. If you are in earshot of negative comments or competition address it clearly, positively and firmly. There are ways of doing that and making clear behaviour is unacceptable without embarrassing anyone – whether by asking the right questions, overruling what you've heard and explaining why, or taking someone aside and talking to them privately. All of that is easier if you have clearly articulated values and behaviours, otherwise someone may take it personally.

## We all want to feel valued

If you have a team which is struggling to get along with each other it can be useful to address it openly on an away day. I've facilitated days with unhappy teams who just wanted to feel heard - by each other and by the leaders of the organisation. Give people a chance to constructively air how they felt and what they would like to see change, and then encourage them to take responsibility for taking the culture themselves rather than acting like victims.

A really simple exercise around what makes people feel valued can be really helpful too. Often we assume that everyone is like us on some level and therefore, if we like attention or freedom or seniority, then we assume that everybody else does too. As a result we end up trying to motivate people using completely the wrong methods.

And we also have unspoken rules around behaviour. For example, if you are consistently late for meetings with me and then cut them short then it feels like you think you have more important things to do and I find that very demotivating. But other people don't feel like that and often run late and would have no idea that I am reading so much into their actions.

Create a safe space so that no-one feels attacked and ask everyone to share one thing that makes them feel unvalued and one thing that makes them feel valued. You will learn a lot about your team and about how best to manage and support each of them as well as what not to do. Some people feel super valued if you make them a cup of tea, which I would never think of doing as I don't drink tea or coffee. Some people love autonomy whilst others love freedom – there is no one right way to make people feel valued so why not ask people instead of working it out by trial and error?

Jenni Anderson of Haven House on how she tackled the situation where income sits between two teams…

*"What we raise as a team – the bottom line - is more important than whose income line it shows in. I am clear that our culture should not be about saying "That's mine". We set some values that say "This is how we're going to operate together; we're going to help each other out, we're going to let each other know when we're busy and we don't want to be disturbed, we're going to let each other know when we're a bit stressed". Sometimes some things are not going to work as well and others will and we'll celebrate those things together. More importantly, it shouldn't matter to the children we're looking after what 'line' that income sits in. The focus should be on them."*

# TEAM BUILDING

**What makes a team?**
Great teams share a sense of purpose – they're in it together. They share a culture, a way of doing things and treating each other. They're all pulling in the same direction and everyone has a place and feels valued. A great fundraising team knows that raising money for the cause is more important than which cost centre the income goes in and any competition is friendly and healthy. A great team encourages those who are struggling and pitches in when someone is overwhelmed with work. They're interested in each other's work and can't wait to share and celebrate their successes.

**Creating a great team**
Sometimes you're lucky enough to inherit a great team when you join a charity. In that situation your role is to understand the team culture as well as possible and find your role within it.

- Spend time observing how people communicate with each other, and with you and why it works
- See if you can collectively capture the values and behaviours that drive the culture – that will help you induct other new people into the team in the future
- Adapt your leadership style to the team and organisation rather than sticking to how you have always done it – the last thing you want to do is disrupt a team that is performing well
- Be careful with how you give people your time and attention – make sure you're not biased towards particular people or areas as that can create tension

Sometimes it is your role to create a better sense of team and get everyone working together more effectively. So where do you start? There are some formal things you can do to create a team culture and you'll find those in the chapter on Creating Your Culture.

## Team formation model

If you are creating a new team, or bringing new members into your team it can be helpful to know that there is a process that many teams go through. There is a model called Tuckman's stages of group development and it says that teams go through 4 stages – Forming, Storming, Norming and Performing.

**Forming** – people are polite and friendly whilst they get to know each other. The leader tends to play a more dominant role and some team members may feel anxious about the new situation.

**Storming** – tensions arise as people push against the boundaries, experience personality clashes as they approach things differently and everyone wants to know where they stand in this newly formed team. If people are unhappy, they may question your authority or the effectiveness of the new team.

**Norming** – people settle down into their roles and get to know each other better.

**Performing** – people are now performing well together and need much less of your time and attention.

It can be reassuring to know about this process if your team is in the storming phase and it can also be helpful to understand that your team will need you less once they are working well together.

## The informal bit

There is also a lot you can do informally to build a team by creating the right environment. Researchers at MIT's Human Dynamics Laboratory have found that social conversations outside of formal meetings are vital to team success. Their experiments showed that social time turns out to be deeply critical to team performance, often accounting for more than 50% of positive changes in communication patterns, even in a setting as efficiency-focused as a call centre.

Getting your team spending time together outside of formal meetings can make a big difference to the cohesiveness of your team. Open plan offices (and limiting use of headphones for when you need quiet time) are an effective way to encourage face-to-face interaction, and people pick up what's going on around them. I worry about fundraising teams when I walk into their offices and it is deathly quiet. Fundraising is a relationship-based job for many income streams and we should all be talking to each other and on the phone to supporters rather than relying too much on email.

I've always sat in the open office because it allows me to be part of the team, hear what is going on (the good and the bad) and get to know people better. It's also lonely in an office on your own (though handy for meetings). In small and medium sized organisations, I would encourage fundraising leaders to sit with their team rather than in a separate office.

Here are some simple ideas that I've seen work well…

- Lunch/breakout area
- Sofas where people can sit and chat in a less formal setting
- Picnic lunches where everyone brings some food and you all eat together or teams take turn to host the lunch
- Walking meetings and meetings outside in the park in summer
- Social committees who plan monthly activities
- A buddy system for new staff members
- A power walking lunchtime club
- Volunteering together

Alan Gosschalk on how he encouraged team building at Scope …

*"Obviously we want people within specific teams to support each other, and they're likely to be closest to each other – as opposed to people in other teams - but then also we get people socialising together to feel like a whole Fundraising division. There's a softball team, which is mostly made up of Fundraising and External Affairs staff. I also organize a work-choir, and there's a concrete garden up here and some people have formed a gardening club. There's a cocktail club that people go to about once a month. There are quite a lot of fun and different things that people can engage in. Work needs to include some fun. People work pretty hard and are under pressure and so having some fun is a vital release.*

*I've always done a lot on the social side and on celebrating success, for example. We have 'Fundraiser of the Month' here and you can nominate your colleagues for going above and beyond in their job or putting some of the five Scope behaviours into action. The winner gets a £10 M&S voucher and a little cup to put on their desk for the month and people absolutely love it. Those sorts of things are really important in getting people to feel like they are a team with a communal aim."*

# MANAGING REMOTE TEAMS

Leading a team and creating a consistent culture is a bit easier if all of your team are based in the same office. When you have remote teams or individual remote workers you need to put extra thought into how you include them in your team's activities, and not just the work activities.

**Put yourself in their shoes**
The best place to start is to think how you would feel if you were based outside of the main hub of your organisation. Do they feel included or isolated? What are their relationships like with those members of the team that they don't work with directly? Are they getting the information that you are communicating informally to those sat around you and the same encouragement and support? Are any of your motivation tools (like a whiteboard with targets and progress on it) leaving them out?

I haven't worked in a remote office myself but I have managed remote teams and I found that I needed to make a conscious effort to consider them in the way I led the team and managed my direct reports. They reported that they had felt neglected in the past and under-valued and I did my best to change that but I'm not sure I always managed it. That is why I was really interested to ask Kate Collins about how she and her fundraising management team at Teenage Cancer Trust kept their regional fundraisers engaged, as they always seem super enthusiastic to me…

*"Not always perfectly, would be what I would say. All my answers have to be qualified with that, that I haven't quite worked it all out yet and I'm not sure if anybody has. If they tell you they have, they might be stretching the truth. But when it comes to dispersed teams you need to deliberately engineer the things that happen more naturally when you're all working in one place. So when I was Head of Regional, I spent a lot of time on the phone and I used to make sure that Fridays in particular would be the day I checked in with people. You phone them up and give them a space to download about their week or tell you about something they probably didn't think was exciting enough to email you*

*about, but is something they really want to tell you about. Often those are the most important things.*

*It's also good to get people together as a whole team or as a regional management team and we find that arranging a creative session or a bit of an update session the day before allows people to stay over and be sociable. You have to be quite a lot more deliberate about engineering casual social interaction because otherwise it doesn't happen and fundraisers, I think by their nature, love contact."*

**Talk to them about it**
The best way to find out how your remote workers feel and to find out how you can improve things is to ask them. You can do this directly, or if you feel that people will be reluctant to sound negative then you could use a staff survey, which would allow them to comment anonymously.

Ask them questions about how much they feel part of the team, what makes them feel valued and unvalued and how they think that you personally and the organisation can improve the situation. If you have created a culture of encouraging people to come with solutions, not just problems that should help avoid a long list of moans. And if they have a long list then you've got lots of work to do!

Here are some things to think about when working with remote teams…

- **Bringing the team together** – consider the practicalities for remote workers when you bring the whole team together. Make sure that they don't have to get up at the crack of dawn and that they have the option (but not an obligation) to stay overnight so that they can spend some time with the team socially.
- **Embed culture** - Get really clear on your culture, values and behaviours so that remote teams have a clear sense of how to work together and with you and don't develop their own sub-culture.
- **Recruitment** – when hiring people who work remotely make sure that you check that they understand what their day to day working environment will be like and that they are able to motivate themselves and be self-sufficient. Fundraisers are sociable people and can find it hard working alone.
- **Invest time upfront** – when you start in the role make it a priority to meet remote workers in your first few weeks and get to know them. They will feel neglected if you've been there a month and you've not made the effort to meet them.
- **Visit regularly** – it may not to be practical to visit often if you have a number of remote teams but set a regular schedule for visits

and stick to it so that the team know when to expect you. Set realistic expectations about your communication schedule.
- **Experience a team meeting from their perspective** – if your remote workers dial in to team meetings, then attend a meeting from their office and see how well it works from a distance. It should give you plenty of insight and ideas on how you can improve things for virtual attendees.
- **Operate a virtual open door policy** – if you have an open door policy where anyone in your team can chat to you when they want to them make sure that you regularly remind your remote workers that they can have the same access to you by phone or skype.
- **Acknowledgement** – when you're writing reports, sending emails etc. make sure that you take the opportunity to acknowledge the work of remote workers by name so they feel loved.
- **Plan for social interactions** – as Kate Collins mentions in her interview, you need to deliberately engineer the things that happen more naturally when you're all working in one place. When you speak to remote workers on the phone, take the time to chat socially for a while first rather than getting straight down to business. Either create a buddy system or ask team members in your main office to call their remote colleagues every now and then to say hello and see how they are doing. Put more emphasis on the social side of away days then you would do when you're all based in the same place.
- **Be watchful** – how will you know if a remote worker is unhappy? It is often quite subtle and easier to pick up when you see people all the time. Keep an eye out for signs like lateness and missing deadlines and ask people how they are feeling.

Jenni Anderson of Haven House on keeping in touch with her retail team…

*"I have a Head of Retail who manages our retail team. They are remote workers and this comes with challenges. Investing the time in visits is important, but we've only got four shops. If we had 20 shops, would that be a realistic thing to do as a Director of Fundraising? Probably not. Those staff, who are working incredibly hard, may then only see you once a year. As a Director who sees her team on a daily basis, that feels like an anathema to good team working."*

# COACHING YOUR TEAM

Unlike mentoring where the mentor shares their knowledge and experience, coaching works from the assumption that individuals have all the answers themselves and just need to be asked the right questions to help them access a new perspective and approach.

The benefits of a coaching approach are that it empowers those receiving coaching to think for themselves, find solutions and take a positive, proactive approach to improving themselves and their performance. Coaching is best seen as a positive investment in an employee to help them fulfil their potential, rather than a way of dealing with poor performing employees.

Some charities hire a highly trained external coach, as Catherine Miles describes below. Other charities commit to developing a coaching approach to line management and train managers to use coaching as a tool for line management. Learning some coaching techniques can be really helpful for any manager or leader. Even just knowing some good questions to ask to help a direct report shift their thinking or become more self-aware can be really powerful. There are plenty of courses out there that can teach you the basic coaching techniques.

Coaching has to be based in trust as it requires coachees to be honest about what might be holding them back. That can be really hard to share with your line manager and in fact you might be the problem sometimes! It can also be hard for line managers to think like a coach i.e. impartially and committed to the development of the coachee as a priority, rather than thinking like a manager with their own agenda and pressures to deliver results. For that reason I suggest finding a few coaching tools that help you to bring the best out of your team but not trying to run formal coaching sessions with individuals unless you've had a lot of training.

In my interview with Catherine Miles she shared how Anthony Nolan used coaching with their team with great results...

## Where does coaching fit in with your approach to fundraising?

My sister is a learning and development coach, so we always had lots of chats about what coaching was and what it did, and then I started working with a coach who actually is now our coach in our division, and I found it really useful. Our coach is trained in solutions-focused coaching, and I felt there was a really nice intersection between the theory of solutions-focused coaching and fundraising, because fundraisers tend to be practical – it's about how to handle a particular situation better so I get an outcome that I'm looking for.

We did Insights profiling as an organisation first, and I thought Insights was really interesting. We started doing Insights profiling with the whole of the division - so now every time somebody starts, they do an Insights profile and they get a 1 to 1 feedback session with the coach. We also use Insights profiling to look at how the teams work with each other together, with colleagues within fundraising and outside of fundraising. I think it depersonalises things and gives everyone a bit of a safe shared space, particularly when you look at where everybody is in the overall divisional wheel.

## Out of interest, what colours were prominent? (Insights profiles people by colour)

Like a lot of fundraising teams we have a fair amount of reds and yellows, and more greens than we thought we had. At that stage I'd been trying to do some training sessions where I'd very much been talking at people - death by PowerPoint. Things were moving a bit, but I wasn't quite getting the full response that I wanted, and when I sat down with the divisional wheel with my coach, I realised "Oh my god, this is why it's not working. We've got a whole bunch of earth greens who really don't like change and are worried about change, but won't tell you they're worried about change - so they're sitting there nodding politely during these sessions but not then putting it into practice." I was doing it as a red would, i.e. "Here's the factual information, now go and put it into practice", but actually, what greens need is to understand and emotionally want to commit to doing it and know that they're going to go on that journey. So we completely changed how we were doing the training and we do things in a very, very different way now.

I think Insights has that mix of the intellectual background and robustness and it creates a common language, a shared space. You can imagine when new people start and we're all talking about colours they worry they've joined some sort of cult! We used to do the profiles very early, and then we realised it could feel a bit weird in your first couple of weeks if you got asked to do this. We give people a few weeks now, and then we show them what a profile looks like and are clear they don't have to do it. It's always done in a supportive way, but also it's quite a big thing, because you do literally get this 12 page report, and some people really don't like it and feel that they're being put in a particular box. We never make someone undertake the profiling if they're uncomfortable – it's totally voluntary.

**And how do you structure the coaching?**
We provide 6 sessions of 1 to 1 coaching for different fundraisers at different times. There are always coaching goals set with their line managers and there are 3-way meetings between the coach, the fundraiser and the line manager at the start and the end of the process. So they're always working on specific things about their personal development, but we particularly use it if people are stepping up into management positions for the first time, or stepping up to head of team, or if that team is working on something particularly big. We use it as a really intensive support mechanism when there are really huge things going on in people's careers. Those sustained 90 minute sessions are always very practically focused around what they need to be doing with their supporters. And you have to have the right coach that fits with your team, because if people just don't like them, it just doesn't work.

**How are you justifying the investment internally, because as a coach, I would love to see more charities investing in coaching?**
Not every charity is going to do it. I think it is really reasonable compared to external training programmes. It's tailored and it gets results so I think it's great value for money. I suppose we've also been very fortunate that as a charity, most of the Anthony Nolan directors have coaches, so it's very much something that goes on within the charity. The Chief Executive supports it and she has an HR background, so that helps as well.
Each time we've requested investment we've specified the things we'd like to do, and obviously we've always fed back on results, and we can show it's really driving tangible benefits, so we've been able to make a very strong business case.

We've always done things gradually too. One of the things we also did with the coach was 6 sessions over 6 months of advanced coaching and leadership training for myself and the heads of fundraising. We felt that was useful in terms of our own management and leadership styles, so we then did a different bespoke version of that course for the management tier below us, and that group included people who might be moving up into management. You know, that classic thing that charities never do - they never pre-train people. They plonk them in and 9 months later you might send them on a course after their lack of management experience has led to problems. So we were trying to build in that future capacity.

Our HR team can see that our staff turnover is better than the sector. They can hopefully see evidence of good management practice, and of course they give us a huge amount of support as well on that. We do the "Best places to work survey", and the fundraising team has come out as a 3 star division every year we've done it, and we've always been ahead of the overall organisational score so the HR team can see quantifiable evidence of a high performing team where actually there's lots of good investment in staff development going on. If we weren't growing income and delivering our most important role for the organisation, then the conversations probably would be quite different.

# COACHING YOUR VOLUNTEER FUNDRAISERS

Times are changing in fundraising and we need to put ourselves in our donors' shoes a lot more than we currently do. To us wealth screening is an essential tool to identify potential major donors, but to your average donor the idea that we have been profiling them to see if they could give more might be disappointing. We need to raise large amounts of money to pay for the great work our charities undertake but it is hard to do that in a way that feels personal on a mass scale. And our internal fundraising infrastructure often isn't flexible enough to be able to support individuals who are passionate about a cause and want to raise funds in any way they can.

So my radar is always on for approaches to fundraising that feel genuinely donor focused. I interviewed Catherine Miles when she was at Anthony Nolan and was absolutely fascinated by how her community team supported individuals who wanted to raise funds for them.

## Anthony Nolan Case Study by Catherine Miles

I was particularly interested in the major gifts side, which has become a theme of what I've done as a Fundraising Director. When I decided I was ready to move up to Fundraising Director level and started to look for jobs, I was particularly keen on fundraising for charities where people have a personal connection to the cause. I was very interested in whether I could apply major donor theory to all areas of fundraising i.e. relationships with all supporters, whether those supporters were recruited by mass channels or individually.

Obviously, lots of people are very passionate about lots of different causes, but some of the strongest connections in the sector are in health charities, and of course Anthony Nolan supporters have a particularly strong connection to our cause because we play a direct role in people's treatment. We actually find you the stem cell donor that saves your life.

I was very interested in how you can take a charity that's got a fantastic case for support, but is raising less money than it should. A charity that certainly seems to have loads of potential, and loads of passion and enthusiasm and commitment amongst the supporters it has, but perhaps isn't fully harnessing that. And how can you actually have proper relationships with those supporters? How can you really understand what their motivations are, really talk to them about how they want to give money to the charity, or how they want to fundraise, and also all the other different non-financial ways they want to support?

That classic meta data approach of not looking at people in silos, not looking at people as cost centres, but actually thinking, "What is this person interested in, how might they like to help us, and how do we facilitate that, whether that's volunteering or campaigning, or awareness raising as well as giving and raising money?" I was very interested to see if you could actually put that into practice, or if it all becomes too difficult.

What we've tried to do is essentially implement major donor fundraising with community sources. I always had this theory that people generally in your community program are classic worker bees. They're people who proactively come to the charity and say, "I want to do some fundraising for you", and generally they've got a pretty good idea about what they want to do. They tend to be people who are very sociable, very energetic, and the sort of people who make things happen. I think we all know this, but somehow the charity sector started to view those people as providers of unsolicited cash. "These people will just do these things, we'll give them a fundraising pack, and they'll do all their bake sales, and we can just let them do that and then thank them for the donation."

What I felt was there was something much, much stronger and much more exciting there. That actually if you were energized enough to get onto a website or pick up a phone and say to the charity, "I want to raise money for you," you probably had a personal reason for doing it and the drive to make it happen, and I always felt there was probably an enormous amount of untapped passion and commitment and enthusiasm about those people.

Essentially what we did was restructure our community fundraising programme from the regional fundraising managers who were based all around the country. We centralised that in two moves. We did one restructure and then another restructure and we have a team of relationship managers in London covering supporters across the UK.

They don't have any products, they don't divide their portfolio of supporters that they work with by type of activity. You don't have a fundraiser working on schools for example. They divide them based on financial potential - so exactly like a major donor programme would. When people get in touch with us that first phone call is absolutely key. We essentially ask them coaching questions about what's motivating them to support us, what sort of fundraising do they enjoy doing, who have they got who might be able to help them with the fundraising and who are they connected to?

All this amazing stuff comes out about why people want to raise money for us, and we enable people to realise they can raise more money than they ever thought possible. It's amazing what opportunities people have access to that they don't realise. We have very close relationships with them, do a lot of the classic type of major donor cultivation work and support them all the way through their fundraising, but also whatever else that they're interested in doing, whether that's awareness raising or volunteering.

What we find is of course is that people are raising phenomenally more than they would do otherwise, and interestingly they're going out and getting other people involved, so they're almost running mini local fundraising campaigns. So there's this massive cross-feeding of all the programs, because they're essentially acting as like ambassadors, which is fantastic.

We've had more than ten £100,000 plus relationships and something over 50% of the net income comes from the top 50 supporters, so we're essentially getting fundraising campaigns that are actually at major gift level. And they go on and support us year on year and they are great news advocates for us, doing press and PR. There's a very interesting cycle you sometimes you see where they have a very intense burst of fundraising, then they go through a period where perhaps they're doing some volunteering for the charity, and then a couple years later they come back to fundraising again.

It's pure relationship fundraising basically. It's about having those multifaceted relationships. That's very interesting, and it's because we're not trying to silo them, and also we're not trying to force them down a particular activity, whereas I think a lot of charities where their community fundraising programme is very product-based, if somebody gets in touch with them, I think there's a natural inclination to say "Do our cake sale at work in December".

It also means that we have to work very cohesively across the organisation and across the fundraising division. Particularly when we have patient appeals, which is when someone (typically a child) urgently needs to find a stem cell donor, and a family will contact us, and there will be a very, very intensive period of public awareness. It'll often be very driven by social media, and it's very much the family leading those appeals. Those can either have very intensive bursts of publicity, or people joining the stem cell register, or people raising money, or people doing a combination of all 3. What we have there is very sort of loose and flexible - like little project teams from across the organisation.

We have a patient appeals summit and that involves all of the people across the organisation who might be touchpoints for patient appeals. So our patient support teams, our donor recruitment staff in the field who sign up the stem cell donors, right through to our press team, and our social media team, because of course often the first time you spot things is when something just pops up on Twitter, and you have to respond very fast. We try to understand a bit about what are the families going through, where they are in that transplant journey, and then we work out the best way for us as an organisation to support them. There's always one main point of contact with the family, which tends to be the team where the family arrived in the organisation first and then behind that, there's always this sort of loose group of representatives from all the relevant teams that are involved.

You can imagine how many press enquiries can come hurtling in to the family and one of the things we try to do for them is help field those press enquiries, because it can become a huge news story very, very quickly. The media pressure can be very intense and these people are in the middle of an incredibly traumatic period of their lives. We've learnt with some of the very, very big ones how quickly we need to respond, how closely we need to coordinate internally, so usually during those periods, little project team will meet every day even if only quickly. Then over time things will calm down.

It's amazing what people can achieve for charities in a very, very short period of time in those situations. They can make a massive difference to a cause and they can build these extraordinary social media audiences. I think there's a really interesting journey that the patients and their families at the heart of those stories go through. It can be exhilarating and uplifting, and they can feel a huge amount of public support, but then the flip side of that is you've also got the public scrutiny at an incredibly traumatic time, and of course you can also get your 1% of the population who starts behaving like trolls on social media. Our role is to support people as much as possible.

I think there's a very interesting thing for charities working with those patients around always making sure, which I think Teenage Cancer did incredibly well with Stephen Sutton and his family, that the appeal is actually being owned and driven by the patient and their families themselves. Even if there are opportunities coming up that would be big, high-profile ones, it's really, really important that the family feels in control, that they're driving, and that they're deciding what they do and what they don't do. I think sometimes some charities find that nuance difficult in the heat, and particularly where things move so fast with social media.

You can then build those relationships into long-term relationships that evolve into lots of different areas, but you've got to have those relationship building skills internally, and it is so important that the supporter is in control. Too many charities have either got themselves set up in the enormous mass fundraising style, or I think some fundraising teams have a bit of an urge to control rather than give supporters freedom and autonomy.

I think obviously there's logistical advantages from the fact we're all in the same room, but essentially the model we have is that each relationship manager in the community team is looking out for about 200 people at any one time. Some of those relationships, exactly like a major donor programme, will be very active, others will be in the stewardship phase, others will be right at the start. So I think if you were in one of the very big charities that had a huge number of supporters with a personal link to the cause and keep those principles of a relationship manager with a portfolio of supporters they are working with to build relationships and empower people to raise money in the way they want, I think it's absolutely scalable. I think all that happens is you've just got more people doing that with more supporters.

# LEADING VOLUNTEERS

Most fundraising teams include a dedicated team of volunteers who help keep the organisation going, whether by working in the office, helping out at events or running committees. I've seen some teams involve volunteers wonderfully and other teams where the needs of volunteers and their role in the team weren't really considered.

## Motivations
Much of leading is based on motivating people but the motivations of volunteer are far more varied than those of the staff team. Volunteers are there for any number of reasons. Many have a very personal connection to the cause as a beneficiary or because the charity has supported a loved one. Others want to be part of their local community. Some people want to feel useful or less lonely after retiring. Some people are looking to gain experience in the sector and new skills to make them more employable. And others love events and want to be part of a team and make a difference. My point is that unless you ask each of them individually then you won't understand how best to make them feel valued and make sure that their experience fulfils their needs as well as the organisation's needs.

## Audit your volunteering programme
It is a good idea to audit your volunteer programme every few years to make sure that it is as effective as possible. You should consider anonymous surveys, focus groups of volunteers and asking staff for their input. You could look at the following areas...

- **Recruitment** – are you recruiting enough volunteers? Do they have the skillsets you need? Can they work the hours you need? Where are you finding your most skilled volunteers? Why do people want to volunteer with your charity? Is your recruitment meeting equal opportunities guidelines?
- **Retention** – how long do volunteers stay? What makes them want to stay? Why do they leave? Do they tell you they are leaving or do

they just drift off?
- **Job description** – how accurate are your job descriptions for volunteers? Do they need to be updated? Do you need to create some specialist volunteer roles?
- **Task appropriateness** – do you have enough relevant tasks for your volunteers? Are they twiddling their thumbs? Do they end up waiting on staff for input? Are the tasks meeting their needs in terms of experience and enjoyment?
- **Support & line management** – are you offering enough support for your volunteers and is it the right kind of support? Do they each have someone who line manages them and looks after their welfare? How much time is supporting volunteers taking? Could that be made more effective?
- **Policies & procedures** – do you have all the policies in place for working with volunteers? Do you have procedures outlined for the main volunteer tasks so that it is easy to brief people and clear what you are expecting? Are your volunteers aware of any legalities around the fundraising they are helping with?
- **Quality** – is the work done by your volunteers of a high quality? If not, what are the issues and how could they be addressed?
- **Thanking** – how often do you thank volunteers? Do you have a Christmas lunch for them? Is there a recognition system for long-term volunteers?
- **Inclusion** – do volunteers feel part of the fundraising team and as valued as your staff team?
- **Practicalities** – do you always have a desk for office volunteers? Do they have access to the stationery they need?

That should give you a list of things that you could do to improve the volunteer experience and the effectiveness of volunteers.

## Making volunteers feel part of the team
Managing volunteers is a job in itself and it is a good idea to have someone who leads on this within your team so that it is considered a priority. This could be a head of a team, someone taking on their first management role (they'll need support) or if you have a lot of volunteers this could be a dedicated staff member.

Invite office volunteers and any other fundraising volunteers who are close to the team to take part in away days – it will provide an interesting perspective which you wouldn't otherwise be able to access. If you have a wall with photos of the team make sure that your volunteers are on there as official team members.

Include volunteers in invitations to social events and make those events at hours that work well for volunteers if possible. As a volunteer it is lovely to be invited into the office because you are liked and part of the team and not just when your help is needed. I am writing this at Christmas and it occurs to me it would be nice to include office volunteers in your Secret Santa.

Recognise the contribution of volunteers wherever possible – on your website and in your annual report and event brochures. You could also have an annual volunteer lunch hosted by you and the CEO. And invite volunteers on project visits so that they can see the difference that they are making.

**Further reading...**
Further information on volunteering can be found on the NCVO website

# TOP COMMUNICATION TOOLS

Ask most people what their biggest complaint is about management at their organisation and they'll talk about poor communication. And yet Fundraising Directors spend a lot of time communicating so how can you do it more effectively? Here are the tools I've seen used most effectively…

**Whiteboards** – whether to celebrate successes, share targets and progress or just leave updates and messages, a great big whiteboard is an invaluable communication tool. At Rainbow Trust we had a whiteboard where we shared all the things we were proud of and as Fundraising Director I made an effort to always chat to whoever was writing their items on the board, giving them a bit of my time and attention. It took a while to bed in but it worked remarkably well.

**Fundraising report** – use monthly reports to communicate to the rest of the team about your activity, successes, upcoming plans and to thank people who've helped you out. Particularly helpful if you're looking to help people understand how much activity is going on and why it matters (or if you need to motivate a manager not achieving much)

**Monthly meetings** – get really focused about how to make the most out of your team meetings. You might want to have a problem-solving sessions, understand each other's biggest challenges and how you can help, teach each other some skills or share stories about your beneficiaries.

**Calendars** – keep them up to date with where you are so that your colleagues can helpfully answer any calls for you when you're away.

**Away days** – a great opportunity to consciously develop team culture, create strategy and have some fun in the process.

**Celebration ritual** – what do you to consistently celebrate success? Why not come up with a ritual. Alan Gosschalk shares how it worked at Scope…

*"We have a thing called Fish, which I never invented, but when there are successes, someone sends around a Fish email. It comes from one of the markets in New York where they chuck these fish at each other, and so when people have successes, they'll email round about those sorts of things. Some teams will do different things, like the events team has got a success chain that they've got a running email that they just add to when they get nice feedback from people."*

**Chat over coffee** – if someone is new to the team, or you're struggling to see eye on eye on work topics why not invest a bit of time in building a relationship with them over a coffee. Or even just start with making them a cup of tea. You'll be amazed by the little things you discover you have in common once you start to spend a bit of time together and how helpful those relationships can be to your working day.

**Understand your colleagues' unspoken rules** – can't stand people turning up late to meetings? Like a bit of small talk before someone launches into a work discussion? Feel valued by someone making you a cup of tea? We all have things which make us feel valued and things which make us feel unvalued. But they're often very different. For some lateness equals rudeness, for others it's just not a big deal. So why not take some time as a team to understand how your colleagues like to be treated and share what makes you feel appreciated? It can help to develop some shared ground rules too like starting and ending meetings on time and not holding non-essential meetings.

**Get sociable** – Alan Gosschalk talked me through the social activities at Scope and you can read more in his full interview at the end of the book.

# CHANGE MANAGEMENT

*"Change is hard because people overestimate the value of what they have and underestimate the value of what they may gain by giving that up"*
James Belasco and Ralph Stayer

Change is a fact of life and happens in all organisations but it is something that people often find hard to embrace, for reasons the quote above describes perfectly. As a leader it is important that you get comfortable with change, and not just the change that you want to create.

There is only so much that you control. Unexpected things happen. You could have the perfect team and culture in place and then two key staff members announce their departure. Or your biggest donor could choose to stop supporting you. The boss you know and love could leave and be replaced with someone you find harder to work with. Your methods for raising your main source of income could come under fire from the media and be subject to regulatory changes. Those are just some of the variables outside of your control and you need to accept that and be ready for when circumstances change.

As a leader you may also need to implement unwelcome changes including culture change, redundancies and restructures. Whether change is planned or unexpected, how you deal with it yourself and how you lead your team through it are important.

**Kotter's 8 Step Change Model**
If you are planning change it is useful to have a model that helps you to embed that change and take people with you on that journey. Kotter's 8 step change model is the best approach to this that I have found.

1. **Create urgency** – demonstrate that there is a need for change to happen and to happen now. Start to talk about the need for change and the challenges and consequences of things remaining as they

are. Make a business case for the change bringing in key stakeholders. Kotter says that for change to work you need to have 75% of people on board with the change so take your time to really get people to that stage before moving to the next step.
2. **Form a powerful coalition** – identify the people who will help you to lead the change and get them fully on board to advocate alongside you.
3. **Create a vision for change** – clarify what the change looks like and what the team or organisation will look like when it is done. Make this a compelling vision with a plan for getting there and a clear picture of the end result that you can share with people. It could be simple – where you are now, where you want to go and how you are going to get there.
4. **Communicate the vision** – share your vision with people. Share it in a formal meeting but also build it into other conversations and communications to really embed it. Give people a chance to discuss their concerns and speak openly about it.
5. **Remove obstacles to change** – make sure you are making it easy for the team to implement the change. Review your systems and structures in the light of the change. Work with people who are resisting the change and praise people who are embracing it. Tackle obstacles quickly when they arise.
6. **Create short-term wins** – these show people that you are on the right track. Don't make the first element of your change programme something long and difficult, instead choose something bite-sized that can act as an inspiring example.
7. **Build on the change** – don't celebrate too soon. Keep taking action to embed change, from evaluating what is and isn't working to looking for continuous improvements.
8. **Anchor the changes in corporate culture** – talk about the progress that you've made as an organisation and the positive impact it is making. Embed the change in your recruitment processes.

It can also be helpful to consider adaptability as an important trait when recruiting. Fundraisers who can embrace change rather than being fearful or unwilling to change will make it much easier for your team to adapt to changing circumstances.

If you're personally struggling with change, have a read of the chapter on Resilience, which has some useful tips. My approach to change is to try and shape it so that it works for me in some way - for example how could this situation teach me something? What can I learn? How can I innovate as a result of this change? If I can't find anything positive then I try and accept it and embrace it – there's no point in fighting a battle you cannot win.

Kath Abrahams of Diabetes UK on managing change…

*"I think you have to be comfortable with a certain amount of ambiguity. You have to like it, I think. If you want to live in a certain world, it might not be the role for you, particularly in the current environment. I often have to give people the comfort and the confidence that it will be okay. Even though I don't know exactly how it will be okay, I do know it will be. It's navigating people through when actually everything around you is uncertain. People look at you to be the one that is upbeat, energetic, whether that's within the team or outside in the rest of the organisation. People want their Engagement or Fundraising Director to be inspired and inspiring. You need to bring that. You need to like that."*

# RECRUITMENT

# SUCCESSION PLANNING

Succession planning is a systematic process whereby organisations identify, assess and develop their employees to ensure that they are ready to take on key roles within the organisation.

Succession planning is all about retention. Not just retention of your fundraisers but also retention of organisational knowledge and retention of relationships with supporters. When you lose a great fundraiser you put at risk the relationships they hold and the organisational knowledge - and you have the headache and cost of recruiting and bedding in their successor.

**The current situation**
As a recruiter I saw great people leaving organisations that they were passionate about because there was nowhere for their career to go within those charities. Even worse they were working in charities where no one had honest and open conversations about development and as a result their managers didn't even know they were looking for other jobs.

Traditionally, fundraisers don't stay long in jobs, with an anecdotal average of 12 months for junior fundraisers, and a bit longer for middle managers. Whilst some fundraisers like variety and new challenges, most people would probably stay in their current organisation if they were happy there and were developed and promoted. So why isn't it happening?

Yes, budgets are always tight at charities and few organisations can create a new position to keep a talented staff member - and it can set a dangerous precedent to do so anyway. And in a small charity it's hard to have a lot of levels that people can move up.

But the way charities approach retention of employees needs to change. Many charities struggle to think long-term generally because of the pressure to raise funds in the short-term and as a result there is no planning ahead. If you're not clear on your organisational priorities for the next 3 years then it is unlikely you will be adequately resourced for them.

HR is often under-utilised as a strategic department as well. HR teams should be partnering with leaders to create long term staff development plans that think beyond training and include retention as a strategic priority.

**Tips on succession planning...**
- **Talk about it** - have conversations with your team about where they want to be in a few years' time and what skills and experience they would like to gather along the way. Sometimes people can surprise you with their secret ambitions and some people also only really shine when they reach the level of seniority that suits them. You may have some great potential leaders in your team just waiting to be given permission to shine and some introverts who have been hiding their light under a bushel.
- **Inspire learning** - have a bookshelf of books on management, leadership, productivity etc that you encourage your team to make use of. Reading can inspire us and can give us new skills and knowledge. I particularly recommend "Playing Big" by Tara Mohr to encourage women to back themselves and fulfil their full potential in the workplace.
- **Spot and develop potential** - look at your team and identify the people who have the potential (and the potential desire) to replace you one day. In a larger organisation that might mean creating a really strong team of managers around you, in a small charity it might be about having a deputy who can share some of your leadership responsibilities and could step up into your role if you left. I created a deputy role when I became a Fundraising Director and it was brilliant for me because I could leave half of the team in their very capable hands and I had a peer I could have honest conversations with about difficult things. She and I helped each other through tricky times and when I left she became a wonderful Fundraising Director and the organisation and team had the stability of being led by someone they already knew and trusted.
- **Use secondments and sabbaticals** to give people an opportunity to learn and have new experiences within the organisation. They'll gain new skills and you'll benefit from the insights they have uncovered from looking at fundraising from a different angle.
- **Get good at internal interviews** – internal candidates can sometimes be poorly treated. Make sure they get the same communication and insight that you share with other candidates via recruiters. And think about the messages you are sending to

internal candidates.
- **Give people development time** – as Jenni Anderson points out in her interview, if you're spending 100% of your time doing your current role how are you going to be able to gain the new skills you need for the next level?

I was really interested to hear how some of the best Fundraising Directors approached succession planning...

Alan Gosschalk on his approach when he was at Scope...

*"I've really encouraged people to either try to get promoted internally or to consider being seconded, both within Fundraising and to other areas. For example, recently three fundraisers have gone into External Affairs. There's quite an active push to recruit internally, thus retaining knowledge and keeping staff longer than the stay of the average fundraiser."*

Mark Astarita on retention at British Red Cross...

*"I think that ultimately the most important ingredient in running a successful team is about managing exceptional people and getting the most out of them by giving them extraordinary opportunities to stretch, hopefully in a supportive environment that never feels unsafe and that matters. People excel when they're in a space where it's exciting, interesting, fun and they're at the edge of the possible. We challenge people to be their best and we look to help them get there. There is not a lot of room for the mediocre in the teams I manage... heck it stands out a mile!*

*We've pretty much home-grown most of our first, second and third tier managers. Part of that is because there's nowhere else where you can do it at this scale or volume if you haven't done it in one of our four or five competitors.*

*In terms of team structure at British Red Cross we have quite a steep pyramid. I have five or six people directly reporting to me, with steep pyramids underneath them. Second tier managers are my next level of talent. I'm always thinking about if someone gets run over by the bus, have I got someone there to replace that person? In the nicest possible way of course! I think I have five people who can replace me easily.*

*Another thing I think is really important is never to be fearful of your position. If you live in fear of your position, if you live in fear of your staff going to do you in or take your role then you're paralyzed."*

Kate Collins of Teenage Cancer Trust shares her thoughts on succession planning...

*"I'm re-reading the 'Happy Manifesto' by Henry Stewart at the moment and it talks about how, in order to retain people who are really good at their jobs, organisations tend to turn them into managers, which they might not always enjoy and has a very different skillset.*

*So in terms of retention, I'd love us to be able to be creative and brave enough to have a path for people who are bloody good fundraisers and don't then have to become managers to progress or be recognised. I certainly look at my team and look at what they do and think 'you're an amazing fundraiser'. So it's a very current thing for me, thinking around 'how do we help people have more internal stretch and collaboration and be a safe place to learn?' And I think sometimes that within your current organisation can be the scariest place to learn, because you can feel so exposed. I think people sometimes feel they need to go somewhere else to do their learning. Reinvent themselves. And it would be great to not have to do that.*

*And I think particularly with a growing organisation it's about making sure we don't lose that technical brilliance. I categorically know I've got people here who are technically better than I'll ever be so how do we let them fly and know that they're making progress without them having to move into management and away from fundraising?"*

And Catherine Miles talks about having the right conversations about development at Anthony Nolan...

*"We have an overt emphasis on people's personal development and we're very open about the fact that we're investing in them for what they'll deliver here, but also equipping them for their future career that might be here or might be elsewhere, and that's okay. It's absolutely fine to have those conversations about where they want to go in their career very openly. I think that hopefully makes it an environment in which they feel like they're being invested in and they want to stay.*

*A lot of fundraising teams I've worked in have had a very weird thing about not being open about that, or everything around learning and development being within either very narrow confines of which training course do you want to go on, or "is this definitely going to help your job right here and now?" Obviously it's important to do that, but it's also about developing the individuals more broadly, which will benefit us in the long run, because the more great fundraisers we're pumping out into the sector, in the long run the better for everybody."*

# ATTRACTING THE BEST FUNDRAISERS

It is often hard, even for the larger charities, to find the right fundraiser for the role they are trying to fill. They need to be ready for the role, fit in with the culture of the organisation, work well with their potential colleagues and, of course, they need to <u>want</u> to work for you.

**Your recruitment brand**
It is therefore really important to put some time and attention into your recruitment brand – both as a charity and as a fundraising team. There are charities I could mention that most fundraisers I know would jump at the chance of working with. That's because their fundraising team has a great leader, is doing exciting things and the charity has a reputation as a great place to work. And because they've let people know about all of that. There are other charities that have a bad reputation that people in the know wouldn't touch with a barge pole. If your charity or team has had a turbulent time and things are turning around then you need to let people know things have changed.

If you want to improve your recruitment brand in the sector consider doing some of the following…
- Speaking at sector and fundraising events to raise your profile and the profile of your team
- Taking part in the Best Companies To Work For surveys
- Undertaking a staff satisfaction survey and sharing the results
- Using LinkedIn to build your profile and network within the sector - connect with fundraisers who are the ones to watch and use Pulse to share your views and updates
- Applying for sector awards for e.g. Best Fundraising Team
- Encourage and incentivise your staff to share the job details with people they know in the sector – a warm and genuine recommendation from someone working in the charity goes a long way.

## Working with recruitment companies

Firstly let me declare my bias here – I was a recruiter of senior fundraisers at Charity People, the specialist charity recruitment company, for a year and then became Managing Director. But before that I had my own concerns and questions about the value of recruitment companies and during my time at Charity People I saw how to make the most of working with a recruitment company.

It would be wonderful if charities were able to recruit great fundraisers easily and didn't have to spend any money on recruiting. However that isn't the world we live in – and at the moment great fundraisers are like gold dust with multiple job offers on the table and counter-offers from their existing employer. When you can't fill a vital fundraising position in a timely fashion, it is costing you money. And if you settle for the wrong candidate because that's all you can find then that is also going to cost you money (and energy which is almost more precious) in the long-term.

A good recruitment consultant knows you well, really understands the job and what you're looking for and also knows their candidates well. If they've been recruiting similar positions for a while then they'll have a great portfolio of candidates they know personally. For fundraising roles I would always recommend a charity-focused agency rather than a more mainstream recruiter as fundraising has many income streams and someone outside of the sector won't understand those.

The ideal route is to find a recruiter to partner with long-term. That way they can build a pipeline of candidates that would fit well within your organisation, you can keep them in the loop before you're ready to recruit and they can offer advice on your job description and positioning of the role. It is tempting to work with multiple recruiters to "spread the net wide". I used to do that and wonder why I got terrible CVs. Recruiters have lots of jobs on their books and lots of candidates to manage too. They have to focus their attention on the roles that they are most likely to fill and if they are one of six agencies they are statistically unlikely to fill it so will spend less time on it. If they are the only agency you're working with they will work incredibly hard to fill the role for you.

It is also worth meeting with your recruiter in person (another reason to just use one). This lets them see the office environment, get to know you better and gets them inspired and excited about the role and the work of your charity. The more they know about you, the better able they are to select the right candidates and brief them before the interview.

**First impressions count**
You may be the one asking the questions at interview but at some level it is a two-way process. You should be aiming to make sure that every candidate really wants the job – then you really get to choose.

- Take the time to make your advert and description of the role inspiring, interesting and appealing. Give salary information or you're just wasting people's time.
- Create a great candidate pack. Too often charities send out job descriptions that were created for internal purposes or cut and pasted from old person specifications. A great candidate pack is visually appealing, gives background on the role and the charity and gives a sense of the culture and personality of the brand. It takes time to create these packs but charities like Teenage Cancer Trust do this brilliantly and I've never given their pack to a candidate and not heard the candidate say "I really want to work there – it sounds like such a good fit for me".
- Consider your essential criteria. If EY (formerly Ernst & Young) don't need their candidates to have degrees, do you? Plenty of great candidates have learnt more on the job than they would have done at university.
- Look after candidates when they come to interview – they're nervous so a warm welcome, a drink of water and a smile from Reception will go a long way to settle them down so you can see the best in them. As will running on time.
- Treat people with respect in the interview. They've taken time out of their day job and no doubt done lots of prep to come and meet with you. I've heard of candidates travelling for hours only to find the interviewer has forgotten the interview and cancelled it. And I know of one interview where the CEO took phone calls (in the room!) during the interview. Obviously those candidates no longer wanted the job and as a recruiter I chose not to work with that charity anymore.
- Feed back about all candidates you interview and do it in a timely fashion.

Mark Astarita talks about the fundraising employer brand at British Red Cross...

*"Our fundraising people strategy is that we are aiming to be the best fundraising shop in the sector. Known to be the best fundraising shop, where people want to come and work for us so that the fundraising brand is really powerful. We give people exceptional*

*development opportunities, we grow exceptional talent and you know what? We know they will go, in time. Even after they've gone we hope they'll always tell others that they loved their time at The Red Cross. The fundraising brand grows as a consequence and we continue to attract talent.*

*Almost twenty of my former fundraisers have gone on to be directors of fundraising. That's the thing I'm very proud about. It's lovely that they think I was important in that because I don't always see it that way. I think they're all exceptional."*

Kate Collins shares how she has been building the employer brand for Teenage Cancer Trust…

*"You need to be able to attract good candidates who will thrive in your culture – those two things are a rare combination. I've been quite deliberately making an effort (particularly after Stephen's Story because Stephen's Story is a remarkable story to tell) to speak at the Institute of Fundraising Convention and other sector events. Because it shows fundraisers who we are, what our culture is like and builds that broader sense of connection around our employer brand."*

# HOLDING GREAT INTERVIEWS

*This is a guest chapter written by Nick Billingham of Charity People.*

Having reached a leadership role within Fundraising, it is highly likely you will have led interviews for your current or previous teams. But are these good interviews? And what is a good interview?

It's quite possible this is something you have never given any thought to, so how do we define a good interview? Ultimately, we want an interview to be a strong assessment of a candidate's potential, whilst concurrently selling the opportunity on offer. After all, what use is an interview that clearly determines that 'yes this person could do the role', if after the process they have decided they didn't really like the sound of it? As you will know, finding fantastic fundraisers can be fantastically difficult. So if you find one, you need to make sure you are also selling them the role throughout the process.

To provide this experience, it's unlikely you will be able to turn up on the day and expect it to take care of itself. It also may mean that the HR-provided generic interview questions won't cut it. It is likely you will need to give it some pre-planned thought. This may mean changing the typical organisational structure of your interview process. If you work for an organisation who generally insists on a three stage interview, speak with your HR Business Partner and explain the staffing crisis that Fundraising operates within.

There may be times where you need to move quickly to secure your chosen candidate. I have worked with candidates in the past who have had up to 4 offers of employment at the same time! Introducing unnecessary stages that add weeks to the process can see candidates pulling out of opportunities. This will obviously be a balancing act; you need the process to be rigorous enough to provide you with a strong assessment but agile enough to ensure you don't lose any potential candidates.

There are a number of different tools you can employ to structure your interview: good cop/bad cop (generally a bad idea), use of an assessment centre (although within a small sector think about how potential candidates might feel about seeing people they know), competency based questions, presentations, unseen tasks (written assessments/budgeting). And in reality, there is no one right answer as to what you should be including.

Each role will be different; the income stream and seniority of the post you are recruiting will impact on how you should structure it. However, for every role I would urge you to think about a few different things:

- What the key factors are in determining whether someone has the right skillset for the role?
- Are my questions biased to someone who understands my sector?
- Would I want to work here after this interview?

Once the above is established you can start to build the structure of your interviews and decide on what different tools you will utilise. At this point, think about how much work you are asking of candidates and whether or not it is something you would have been willing to do when you have been looking.

Having identified what type of skillset you need and which assessment tools you are going to use, it is worth revisiting the CVs of the candidates you will be meeting. You can start to think about the specific questions you want to ask each individual. Paramount to this is understanding the specific part someone played in an achievement. I have probably met 30 people over the years who claim to have been behind the success of the NSPCC's Full Stop Campaign! And in reality all of those people will undoubtedly have played some part in its success. But what exactly did they do? Where were things when they started? And where was it at when they left?

Given my key theme in this article is securing the best talent and ensuring you consistently sell the opportunity when interviewing ,you might be thinking that asking these probing questions sounds somewhat punitive, but genuine interest and enthusiasm can go a long way to alleviating this.

It can be quite common for candidates to waffle when addressing an interview question, and you might feel cutting people off could come across as rude. However there will be times when this is necessary. You need to try and stick to the allocated time and you will have a number of different questions you want to get through. Avoid upsetting candidates by outlining from the outset that there may be times you will cut them off – particularly if they have already given the information you seek.

Candidates waffling is usually down to nerves, but sometimes it can be down to practise. Interviewing well is a skill and generally the more you do it the better you will become. It may be that you meet someone who on paper looks absolutely perfect, but in person gives a poor interview. Try not to discount them immediately. Try and help them to relax, find out when their last interview was (if it has been 10 years this might explain extra nerves) and be more specific than you usually would with your questions.

A candidate who can give a good interview is demonstrating strong verbal communication skills. But what if this was not a factor that was important when you planned exactly what you were looking for? If the role is in no way externally facing then perhaps a traditional interview isn't the best method.

Sometimes you might conclude that a candidate isn't right for a role midway through the interview. Should this happen, don't forget you are representing your organisation, and you never know the person in front of you could turn out to be someone you want to impress in the future. Instead of mentally switching off, try and use the remaining time to gather as much information as you can that you can feedback to the candidate. All the information that you provide will be of benefit to them in their next interview. And by all means keep selling the organisation and what you are trying to achieve.

Interviewing can be great fun, but to be successful it needs to be planned and specific to the role you are recruiting. If you are working with a recruiter they will often have suggestions on how best to manage the interview process. Whilst the process itself is relatively straightforward – I ask questions, you answer - to be most effective there is more to think about and plan than you might have imagined.

# RECRUITING ON CULTURE FIT

The time I spent recruiting senior fundraisers and running a charity recruitment company gave me the opportunity to analyse what makes a successful appointment and why things sometimes go wrong.

It is rare that unsuccessful placements are due to the poor performance of candidates. It does happen but generally interviews and track record give a good indicator of how competent someone will be in the role, assuming the interviewer knows their stuff. Much more frequently there is problem with the gap between expectations and reality when it comes to management style and culture fit. And it tends to be the fundraiser who suffers in silence and the manager doesn't know there is a problem until the fundraiser announces they are leaving.

**When I spoke to the recruiting managers about what had gone wrong I heard things like…**
- They couldn't keep up with the pace
- Their expectations of the organisation were too high
- They weren't formal enough when dealing with Trustees
- They didn't seem to get on with their fellow team members/they weren't a team player
- I'm not sure how they are spending their time
- They were too direct with their colleagues
- They spent too much time chatting and distracting the team
- They weren't very good at working on their own

**When I spoke to the fundraisers who had left jobs or were unhappy in their roles I heard things like…**
- My boss micro-manages me and I feel like I am not trusted to do a good job
- I can't get any time/decisions/input from my manager – it feels

- like my work is not a priority
- There is huge pressure on me to get results and work long hours and I feel stressed
- I don't feel like part of a team and it is lonely
- No-one ever makes a decision so we don't make any progress
- We don't have enough resources
- People don't talk to each other and we don't feel like a team
- The office is too noisy and I can't get my work done
- The charity isn't professional enough
- It feels like working for a company, not a cause

As you'll see from the comments above there is no "right" culture – different people excel in different environments. And because the culture of a charity is unlikely to change, you need to recruit people who will thrive in your culture or who are able to adapt to fit in within their environment.

There's a chapter in this book on creating your team's culture but you still need to operate successfully within your organisation's overall culture and working environment. And before you can recruit to fit your culture, you need to be able to define your culture.

**Defining your culture**
Firstly it is important to point out that you're not looking to recruit clones of your existing team and getting cultural fit right works alongside diversity and equal opportunities, not against it. You're looking for a diverse range of people, but they all need to thrive within your charity.

There are some useful ways to capture and articulate your organisation's culture. The first place to start is your charity's **values**. Whilst sometimes values can feel quite generic, it is possible to create values that truly sum up a culture. For example, formal cultures are less likely to use brave, trust and innovation as their values.

The best values have **behaviours** linked to them. Behaviours allow you to articulate what the values mean to your organisation and provide a really useful practical tool that can be integrated into interviews and performance management.

You can also create a **description** of what it is like to work within your team that could be used as part of your candidate pack. Done well (and with an appealing culture) this can significantly increase the number of suitable candidates you attract for your vacancy.

You could ask your team to describe what it is like working for your organisation. I've created videos in the past and that works well because you can see that people are genuinely happy to be part of the team but some quotes would also work.

**Setting expectations**
Apparently when you're dating, you spend the first 6 months projecting a version of your ideal partner onto them, without really seeing the real person. You also do your best to conform to the ideal that is being placed on you. Eventually however the cracks appear in your perfect image of someone as the real them shows up and you're both a bit disappointed (or delighted if they turn out to be even better than your projection).

Interviewing isn't entirely dissimilar to dating in this respect. Candidates are projecting their expectations around culture onto the job and interviewers are making assumptions about how a candidate would approach certain situations without actually asking them about it. This is why a really important part of any interview process is to get really clear on both the culture of the organisation and the culture that would suit the candidate.

These are some areas to specifically cover in interviews…
- **Size of organisation** – whilst some people can change their behaviour and expectations to suit any organisation, most people tend to be best suited to a certain size organisation. In particular, people moving from large charities to smaller charities struggle with the lack of resources and processes, whilst people moving into larger charities often feel a bit anonymous, having been used to everyone knowing their name. It is worth being clear on expectations when you're talking to candidates moving from a very different sized organisation.
- **Formality and hierarchy** – be sure to articulate whether there are formal elements to the way your charity works and whether it is hierarchical or more flat in structure. At some charities your ideas have value whatever level you are at, at others you practically bow when you see the CEO. Everyone is formal at interview so interviews are not the best measure of how well someone naturally operates within a formal environment.
- **How people interact with each other** – if you have a panel for the interviews, how you speak to each other can give an indication of your culture. The same goes for meeting the team, which can be a useful part of the process particularly if you're recruiting a manager or head of a team.
- **Drive and ambition expectations** – if you're looking for

someone who is going to grow income significantly, be sure to articulate that. If everyone works long hours and volunteers at weekends that is important information to share. If you're looking for someone to hold the ship steady and not change things up too much, let your candidates know that.

- **Independence versus collaboration** – some organisations like people who work very independently, whilst in others being too independent makes people feel that you are not a team player. Give examples of when you would expect people to work alone and what sort of things you work on together as a team. I once worked somewhere where everyone in the (small) organisation was involved in every decision, which brought a different quality of thinking to decisions but drove me crazy as I make decisions quickly. There was nothing wrong with how they made decisions but I wasn't a good fit for that organisation.

- **Management style** – this is slightly distinct from culture but it is always good to share your management style (giving examples), ask what style of management brings out the best in candidates and when recruiting managers check that their approach would work with your team and organisation.

- **Office environment** – let candidates see where they might be working. You want them to be able to picture themselves working there and you don't want them to turn up on day one and feel deflated because it doesn't meet their expectations. If you have old computers and crowded desks, find someone who is used to that and not someone who only feels valued with great tech and a lovely environment.

Jools Tait of BEN on how she picks up cultural fit at interview…

*"You have a gut instinct feel of 'do you know what, they will really fit the team' or that they get the sales model. You see their enthusiasm. How they communicate. They're not robotic in how they've prepared for an interview. Also by talk in the interview more about them as an individual and the things they do outside work and what motivates them and where their hobbies lie. Rather than just career skills because they practiced that and mastered that to within an inch of its life.*

*You never go into a meeting and find it 100% what you expect it to be. You've got to be able to think on your feet and engage someone with the organisation, in any situation. An MD, a CEO or whoever is in the meeting, will throw a curveball so in an interview, if you throw those curveballs out, it's also quite interesting to see how people react in that situation. And some people nail it and you know they've got the gift of the gab and you just think, okay they can think on their feet."*

Kate Collins of Teenage Cancer Trust talks about the sort of person that thrives in their culture...

*"I think somebody who believes that fundraising can make a difference to the lives of young people with cancer and is hungry for and comfortable with accountability. Someone who is able to say 'yes I'll make something happen here, but also I'll be accountable for what happened if it wasn't brilliant and I'll learn.' Someone with a really curious mind who asks how they can learn and improve. You can't reverse engineer attitude."*

# RECRUITING FROM THE COMMERCIAL SECTOR

Charities can be very risk-averse when it comes to recruitment, tending to opt for the candidate who has done the job before wherever possible. And when the pressure to bring in the funds is substantial and the budget and time to train staff are insubstantial you can understand why that is the case. But as a result the sector is missing out on the fresh perspective, enthusiasm, commercial approach and contacts that candidates from the commercial world can bring.

As a recruiter I would have daily conversations with candidates from the commercial world wanting to move into the charity sector and do something more meaningful with their careers. And there were very few roles that I could put them forward for outside of a handful of the largest charities that actively recruited commercial candidates for particular teams. As a sector we also lack generic management positions and expect all but the most senior managers to be hands on specialists as well - so there are not many roles that someone with an unrelated skillset can successfully apply for.

The reality is that we have a shortage of great fundraisers, and small and medium sized charities often have to advertise multiple times to get a candidate they actually like. So it is time to get creative about how we bring people into the sector and how we train them as fundraisers.

**Here are some things to bear in mind when recruiting from the commercial sector...**

- Every commercial candidate will talk about their **transferable skills** but you need to understand which skills transfer across and which need to be adapted. An ability to build rapport and relationships and to anticipate and meet a customer's needs is completely relevant but making a sale in the commercial world can

be very different from making an ask in the fundraising world. The better you can articulate the differences (or ideally they can, having done their research), the more expectations will be aligned.
- Ensure that the candidate is not wearing **rose-tinted glasses**. I have met people who moved to charities from the corporate world and expected everyone to be super-nice all the time and for there to be no tensions. Organisations by their very nature have tensions and challenges - and charities are no different. And yes, people choose to work in this sector to make a difference but that doesn't mean that they can't be grumpy, negative and unhelpful at times – they're only human. Make sure that your candidates have realistic expectations about the fact that this is still a job and it will have frustrations as well as satisfaction and the feel good factor.
- Talk **long-term goals** with candidates from the commercial sector. I have seen a lot of commercial candidates take a first job in fundraising at a big salary drop and then expect to move up to Director level (and closer to their old salary) very quickly. Exceptional people can do that (from within and outside of the sector) but if someone's performance is average then they won't be moving anywhere very quickly. Sharing a typical career path within your organisation can help candidates understand the timeline for getting back up to their former salary levels.
- Think about how you can **train** a candidate who has lots of potential but doesn't yet understand fundraising. Think beyond courses – who could they shadow? What do they need to learn? What could they read? Could you introduce them to a mentor? What do you wish someone had sat down and told you about fundraising that isn't written in any text book?
- Ask commercial candidates what **research** they've done to understand fundraising and what they think the role involves on a day to day basis. A great candidate will have spoken to people in fundraising as well as read relevant books, articles etc. I'm amazed how many candidates haven't even done basic research on what their chosen new career involves. I once interviewed for a candidate for a corporate fundraising role who had no idea whatsoever what was involved in corporate fundraising!
- When you've recruited someone from the commercial world be sure to **be open** to what they can bring. That external perspective won't last long so ask them lots of questions about their first impressions and how they would approach the same tasks in the corporate world.

I think the sector would really benefit from bringing in people with different experience and new perspectives so perhaps it is time to look at how we fundraise and whether we can be more commercial about that.

# INTERNAL RELATIONSHIPS

# MANAGING UPWARDS

You may have a team to manage but sometimes managing upwards can be the hardest part of your job. Your team will be looking to you to secure the resources and decisions they need from your line manager, so it is worth investing time in building a strong and mutually respectful relationship with your manager.

**Understand what is expected of you**
It is always a good idea to clarify with your boss what they are expecting from you. Make it part of your induction to download that from them covering topics including…

- What in their opinion are your **main priorities** for the next 3, 6 and 12 months?
- Where do they think the **greatest opportunities** for growth are in your area?
- Which areas do they think will be the most **challenging** and do they have a preferred way for you to tackle them?
- How often do they want to **meet with you** and what format will that meeting take?
- What communication would they like from you in **between meetings**? Would they prefer that you email them as things come up or save it all up for one email or meeting?
- What level of **problem** do they want to know about and what are you okay to deal with yourself and tell them what you did?

**Understanding your manager**
The main secret to influencing anyone is to understand that individual as well as you possibly can. There are things you can ask them about themselves but many people aren't self-aware and you can learn almost as much by watching and listening to how they deal with you and others. Here are some things to look out for…

- What seems to **stress** them out or make them anxious? Most otherwise calm CEOs will get stressed in the run up to Board

meetings for example. Watch for the body language, tone of voice and the words they use that give you a clue that they are not happy – then you'll be able to pick up when you are saying or doing things that are sending them in that direction.
- What are their **bug bears**? For some people it is typos – if you send something to them with a typo in it then they start to doubt your ability to deliver on the detail of everything. For others it might be perceived negativity or not listening enough – listen out for what your manager complains about when they are talking about other people.
- What are they **passionate** about? What do they talk about with the most energy and enthusiasm?
- **How do they their information**? Do they like stories or charts? Are they a visual person who sketches out ideas? Do they make lists? Do they want to go into the detail of everything or do that find that boring and want big picture thinking?
- Are they **risk averse** or do they like to innovate and push boundaries?
- If you use a **personality profile** like Insights or Myers-Briggs in your organisation then ask your manager about their profile and share yours.

Invest in your personal relationship with your manager. It is always nice to start with a lunch where you can chat about things other than work as well. Your manager is human just like you, with a whole life and other priorities outside of work, even if it sometimes doesn't feel like it. Taking the time to remember their children's names or ask about their hobbies shows that you care about them and builds rapport.

### Helping your manager get the best out of you
- Make sure that you **understand what your manager wants you to do** when they delegate a task. It is helpful to reflect back to them what you heard them ask for and ask any clarifying questions you need to.
- Share with your manager what motivates you and what makes you **feel valued**.
- Even if your organisation doesn't routinely use personality profiling you could **share your profile** if you have one or suggest that as a leadership team you all get profiled so you can work even more effectively together.
- If you need input from your manager then share with them **what you need**, by when (and why if necessary).

## Influencing your manager

There may be times that you and your manager do not agree on the best way forward on a particular issue. It is important to find a way to disagree with your manager that is professional, constructive, persuasive and shows appropriate respect for authority. How you do that is going to depend on the individual and what you have learnt about them. Some people appreciate directness, some people like to go away and think about problems and come back to you, some like a good debate and others find it hard to say when they disagree but find another way of showing you.

Timing is also important – if you catch me when I am tired, have sat in boring meetings all day and am hungry, it is likely that I will be less positive than if I am feeling rested and well fed. If you need something from your manager catch them at a good time for them.

Think like your manager. By which I mean understand their priorities and try and consider things from their perspective as well as yours. If you can understand what their concerns might be about a proposal then you can acknowledge those concerns and make counter-arguments. If your manager is the CEO then try and think organisationally rather than just thinking like a fundraiser.

Accept that sometimes you won't get the decision you want from you manager. It is really important to know when you cannot win a battle, acknowledge to yourself that they have more responsibility than you and therefore more authority and accept and make the best out of the decision that has been made.

## Managing yourself

- Consciously decide what i**mpression** you want to give to your manager and keep that front of mind every time you communicate with them. Don't be too relaxed even if they are super friendly – they are still your superior and need to be treated with respect. Sometimes people are not as straight forward as they may appear - people can seem relaxed for example but still judge you for informality in certain situations. My advice is to start cautiously if you don't know your manager at all.
- Be aware of the things you do that previous managers or colleagues may have found annoying and make sure that you **manage your behaviour**. I used to sometimes talk over people when I was really excited about an idea and people can find that disrespectful (and it is - though not purposefully) so now I consciously slow myself down and allow other people more space in the conversation.

- **Stop and think** when you are stressed or worried. If you blast off an email in panic every time something goes wrong rather than reviewing the situation and considering the best approach that will make you seem less in control of your area and yourself.
- Go to your manager with **solutions, not just problems**. It is old advice but still very relevant, particularly for senior staff.

# EDUCATING & ENGAGING TRUSTEES

Relationships with Trustees can make all the difference to the success of your fundraising team and are often a source of tension for Fundraising Directors. If you have a Board that trusts you, will invest in fundraising and understands how to effectively oversee and support fundraising it makes your job much easier. So if you don't have a Board like that what can you do about it?

As ever when trying to encourage someone to change their behaviour, it helps to put yourself in their shoes. Trustees are legally responsible for the charity and a large part of their role is managing risk so they are usually much more risk averse than your average Fundraising Director. New Trustees often don't understand fundraising or only understand a few income streams. If they've been a Trustee for a while they have probably had their fingers burned by a Fundraising Director or investment that hasn't delivered. They're not trained to ask people for money and like most of the population they probably find the idea of doing it themselves an uncomfortable prospect. They donate their time and expertise and take on responsibility and so, quite reasonably, may not see fundraising as part of their role. They may have friends who think face-to-face fundraising is terrible and who believe everything the media says about the evils of fundraising and charities.

As a bare minimum these are the things you want to make sure that your Trustees know about fundraising…

**1. Fundraising is very different from sales (and is much harder)**
Whilst some principles transfer from the commercial world, there is a complexity to fundraising that doesn't exist in sales. You're 'selling' an intangible product and you've got literally thousands of competitors - and they're all good causes.

## 2. If you'd like your fundraising team to raise more money, then you need to change the inputs.

The fact that the charity needs more money doesn't make it any easier to raise more. If you want a significant increase in income then you need to change something. You need to invest in fundraising. Or increase organisational readiness to fundraise. Or get much better at measuring and communicating the need for and impact of your services. A desire to double income isn't enough to make it happen.

## 3. Fundraising isn't a formula

Firstly there are a whole bunch of different income streams. Not all of them will be suitable for your charity. And what works for one charity may not work for another. Yes, there are charities that raise £500k at gala dinners. Because they've spent years building up a network of the great and the good who buy tables and make huge auction bids. And yes, Tesco Charity of the Year raises millions. But writing a letter to Aldi isn't going to get you millions of pounds. You have a worthy cause and you believe in it but (as my Dad would say frequently in my younger years) money doesn't grow on trees.

Your Fundraising Director is an expert at identifying which income streams will work best for your cause. If they gently deflect your ideas, it isn't that they are not listening or being arrogant. It's because they understand their market and they understand your donors and they know why that won't work.

## 4. Trustee involvement in fundraising is crucial

You may not be able to write a big cheque but you could run a marathon, get your company involved, gather together a group of friends to buy a table at an event or introduce the CEO to your next door neighbour's son who happens to work in CSR at a large firm. You already give your time but getting involved in fundraising will make a real difference to helping your organisation reach more beneficiaries. And it will gain you the appreciation of your fundraisers. If you don't feel motivated to give towards your cause then why should complete strangers part with their hard earned cash?

## 5. Fundraising income is hard to predict

It isn't that unusual to start a new financial year with only 20% of your income confirmed. Unless you've invested in individual giving or legacy promotion over a number of years then much of your organisation's income is unpredictable. What can be managed is the pipeline – the number and quality of trust applications, the cultivation events for major donors, the marketing of challenge events, the networking that opens corporate doors. So track the pipeline, read the narrative about variances, identify the point when you should start to worry and, crucially, don't spend money you haven't got.

### 6. Your Fundraising Director is not shameless and money-grabbing

Many people find it uncomfortable asking for money. And understandably a bit anxious about opening up their address book to a Fundraising Director. But your Fundraising Director is not going to storm into a meeting with one of your contacts, skip the chit chat and yell "SHOW ME THE MONEY!!!"

Remember how they built a relationship with you? How they got to know you and asked about your family and your hobbies? Built your trust in them? Kept you updated but didn't pressurise you? Yes you just experienced the subtle art of relationship fundraising and that's exactly how they, and you, are going to engage and inspire your contacts to consider making a donation to your cause.

Now you're clear what you want your Trustees to know, how do you go about getting them truly on board with fundraising? I believe that relationship fundraising starts with your Trustees so rather than taking them for grated and getting a bit frustrated, why not treat them like the major donors they are?

1. **Build rapport** - invest time getting to know your Trustees as individuals just as you do with major donors. How long have they been involved and what drew them to the charity? How is their experience of being a Trustee going? What inspires them and what worries them? Find out about their family, their hobbies, their aspirations etc.
2. **Build trust and knowledge** – make sure that your reports to Trustees are tailored to meet their needs, not your desire to share everything you do. Make them easy to read, highlight key items you need their input on and address any concerns you know they have. Focus on building trust when you present to them, seeing their questions as a positive thing not a criticism. Invite them to events, share materials with them and gradually educate them about the different income streams. You could also produce a monthly update on activity and successes (something I suggest doing for internal engagement too) that they could opt in to receive too.
3. **Find champions** – get a couple of Trustees firmly in your camp so they can influence their fellow Board members as peers.
4. **Build a vision** of what fundraising could do for the organisation and how that will feel for everyone involved.

5. **Thank them** – make sure that you're thanking Trustees for what they do and singing the praises of those who actively get involved with fundraising.

Catherine Miles talks about what it was like working with an engaged Trustee board at Anthony Nolan…

*"I wanted to invest in individual giving and understandably, the trustees were cautious on both reputational and financial grounds, so we spent a lot of time explaining - this is what we understand about how the charity's finances operate, this is what the charity wants to do in future, this is the type of money it's going to need. Actually if we're going to be able to do this sustainably and really have growing voluntary income that really underpins the charity and doesn't fluctuate wildly year on year, we really do need to try and invest in individual giving. Then we had fabulous support from the trustees.*

*I think it probably helped that quite a lot of them are accountants, actually. I think it's that they've always interrogated the numbers in great detail, and scrutinized us incredibly closely. We've always had to report with great frequency, which is absolutely right. It means they really understand what we're trying to achieve in individual giving programme and how it's performing at any given time. They can probably tell you about as much of our individual giving program as I can, which is great, and it's great to genuinely have that partnership, and because they have the finance background, because they've had that level of involvement with us, we can genuinely discuss investment decisions about, okay this channel is now doing this, where should we put our money? That's great and unusual I think as well."*

# INFLUENCING YOUR COLLEAGUES

When you are heading up a fundraising department, some of the most important relationships you have will be with your peers - the directors of other departments. Even heading up particular income streams you will find yourself needing to work effectively with other departments to be successful in your role.

You will be working with your finance team to pull together budgets, improve income-tracking systems and reconcile monthly management accounts. You will be working with your communications team to support your corporate supporters and run integrated campaigns. You'll be working with your programmes team to gather project information and take doors on project visits. And that's just for starters!

In many charities, tensions exist between the various departments, often around similar pressure points. If you are a Director of Fundraising it is your job to reduce those tensions and improve working relationships with other teams. You can't afford to be passive about that – you have to be proactive, as it may well determine how successful you can be in your job.

**When you start**
You have the opportunity to create a blank slate when you are new to the role. Invest time in developing relationships with your peers. Take the time to meet with each of them to understand...

- How their department works
- What their main challenges are
- Where they crossover with your team – what do they need from you and what do you need from them?
- What they think about their relationship with the fundraising team
- How your two teams could work better together

If possible build a personal relationship with your fellow directors (or heads of team if you're heading up an income stream) that will enable you both to navigate tricky times. Take them out to lunch or go and have a coffee together out of the office every now and then. When I start a new role as Director of Fundraising I try to make my Finance and Programmes Directors my new best friends.

If you both come from a place of mutual respect and trust and genuinely like each other, it will make it much easier to resolve conflicts, or even catch issues before they escalate to become conflicts. If your organisation has a culture that values collaboration and sets out behaviours to support collaboration then dealing with inter-departmental tensions will be much easier.

If you come from a place of openness it will encourage others to do the same. Be clear what you need from other teams and what you'd like to change, but also acknowledge where your team, processes and attitude could improve and take responsibility for making that happen. If you understand the objections you may face around any changes you wish to implement then you can prepare a stronger case for change by pre-empting those objections.

You can also use Senior Management Meetings as a place to build relationships. You can build trust by thinking beyond purely fundraising, supporting your colleagues when they bid for more resources and acknowledging what their team does.

**Do your internal PR**
I have lost count of the number of times I have heard fundraising called "a necessary evil" – a phrase that undermines both the donor and the fundraising team who work hard to deliver income. There are a number of reasons that fundraising can get a bad reputation. Often fundraising is misunderstood. Colleagues don't know what fundraising really involves, or how complicated or stressful it can be at times. At worst, all they see is the salaries and the relatively high staff turnover and their experience is often being on the receiving end of requests for information or project visits without any feedback or recognition that they took time out of their busy schedule to help.

In organisations where fundraising is a small part of the organisation's income, it can be hard to get any traction as it is considered low priority. In those situations it is useful to make a clear business case for fundraising, highlighting what voluntary income has paid for over the past few years and what it could fund in the future.

If negativity about fundraising exists in your organisation then you and your CEO need to address it together at Senior Management Team level. A culture where fundraising is part of everyone's job is a helpful goal to have. Your role is to make your fundraising team the best it can be and to work well with other departments but your CEO needs to lead by example and not tolerate negativity about any team to become entrenched in the organisation.

**Communicate**
I think internal communication is a really powerful tool for changing minds and improving relationships. Firstly acknowledge the contribution of other departments – from providing you with a great service, to attending project visits or pulling together a project budget promptly for a funding application. When you are sharing successes at Senior Management Team meetings be sure to recognise any contributions made by your colleagues and their departments. And when you secure a donation as a result of a project visit, the first person to know should be the colleague who showed your donors around the project so that they can feel good about the vital role that they played.

I strongly suggest creating a monthly fundraising report, which is shared with the fundraising team, your CEO and the other directors. This shows everyone exactly what you are doing – helping people to understand more about what you do and how varied and complicated it is. Not everyone will read it but at least they then can't claim that they didn't know about your plans. It also gives you a forum to highlight the contribution of individuals from other teams and thank them publicly. When I've done this in the past it has prompted conversations between teams and even led to recruiting colleagues as volunteer fundraisers for events.

Mark Astarita of British Red Cross on the differences between departments…

*"Many of my colleagues [in other teams at British Red Cross] are rightly focusing on the present. Fundraisers are, by and large, planning, spending and operating in the future tense. What folk will give tomorrow was probably raised many moons ago. So I think we as fundraisers live in slightly different universes to some other parts of our organisations and because almost all our engagement is with the outside world whilst others maybe be more internally focused we may see things from a different perspective.*

*As a fundraiser, your beliefs, and why you're here are just as important as the aid worker or anyone else. You want to change the world, it's just that you've landed on the thing that you can do really well to do that."*

# INNOVATION AND TOOLS

# PURPOSE & DONOR ENGAGEMENT

Let's start by defining purpose in the context of your organisation.

**Purpose:** The difference you're trying to make
**Mission:** How you do it
**Vision:** What the world will look like when you've achieved your purpose

A well articulated purpose statement is simple, inspiring and memorable - unlike many charity vision and mission statements, which can be long and unwieldy.

## How does purpose help engagement?
Purpose feeds into our individual need for meaning and to lead meaningful lives – something that those of us who choose to work in the charity sector prioritise and one of the key drivers for donors making gifts.

Whether it is a true story or an urban myth, I love this story… apparently in 1962 President Kennedy visited the NASA space centre and noticed a janitor carrying a broom. He interrupted his tour, went over to the janitor and said "Hi I'm Jack Kennedy. What are you doing?" the man responded "Well Mr President, I'm helping put a man on the moon".

I also know a property developer who describes his work as "putting a roof over people's heads" and that keeps him motivated. How many people in your organisation, when asked what they do would reply by talking about the cause rather than their job function? How many of them think about it when they go to work every day?

Purpose also provides an emotional connection and influences our decision making. Let's look at a simplified version of how our brains make decisions…

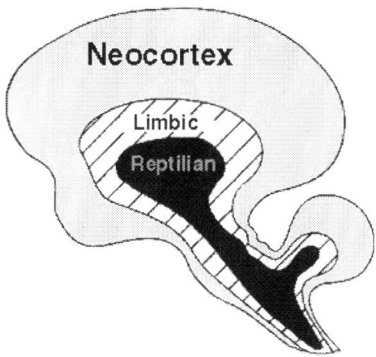

**Neocortex**: This is our newest area of the brain. It is responsible for all our rational and analytical thought and language. This allows us to look through vast amounts of facts and figures, but it doesn't drive behaviour.

**Limbic Brain**: The Limbic brain comprises of the middle two sections and is responsible for all our feelings, such as trust and loyalty. This area of the brain is responsible for all human behaviour and all our decision making. It is where our emotional connection takes place, and it has no capacity for language.

So we make our decisions using our 'gut instinct' and then rationalise them with language using our neocortex. It therefore makes sense to engage people's limbic brain through emotion.

And finally, purpose can give everyone something to get behind – "a common purpose".

### Communicating purpose to engage audiences
Simon Sinek talks about the Golden Circle of communication in his book "Start with Why"...

# The Golden Circle

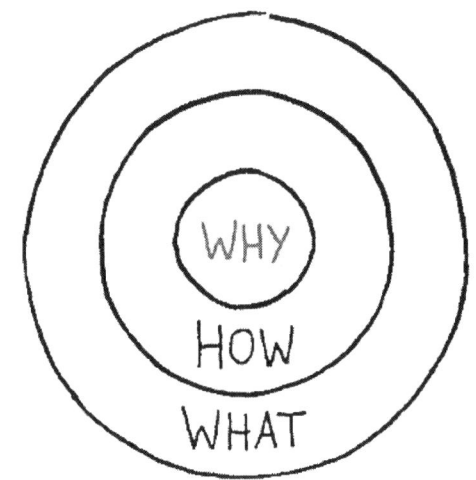

**WHAT**
Every organization on the planet knows WHAT they do. These are products they sell or the services

**HOW**
Some organizations know HOW they do it. These are the things that make them special or set them apart from their competition.

**WHY**
Very few organizations know WHY they do what they do. WHY is not about making money. That's a result. WHY is a purpose, cause or belief. It's the very reason your organization exists.

Sinek argues that being able to articulate your WHY, or purpose, helps organisations to engage their audiences.

Here are some great corporate examples…

**SouthWest Airlines purpose -** *"To democratize the skies – to make air travel as available and flexible for average Americans as it has been for the well to do."*

Purpose: "Southwest Airlines is democratizing the skies."
Mission: "We democratize the skies by keeping our fares low and spirits high."
Vision: "I see a world in which everyone in America has the chance to go and see and do things they've never dreamed of—where everyone has the ability to fly."

It's worth noting that SouthWest Airlines have had 40 consecutive years of profitability, even through 9/11 when airlines suffered hugely. Despite being a budget airline their customer service is legendary and Americans genuinely love them. Ryanair can't say the same thing!

**Patagonia's purpose & brand story** - *"Build the best product, cause no unnecessary harm, use business to inspire and implement solutions to the environmental crisis."*

*Patagonia grew out of a small company that made tools for climbers. Alpinism remains at the heart of a worldwide business that still makes clothes for climbing – as well as for skiing, snowboarding, surfing, fly fishing, paddling and trail running. These are all silent sports. None require a motor; none deliver the cheers of a crowd. In each sport, reward comes in the form of hard-won grace and moments of connection between us and nature.*

*Our values reflect those of a business started by a band of climbers and surfers, and the minimalist style they promoted. The approach we take towards product design demonstrates a bias for simplicity and utility.*

*For us at Patagonia, a love of wild and beautiful places demands participation in the fight to save them, and to help reverse the steep decline in the overall environmental health of our planet. We donate our time, services and at least 1% of our sales to hundreds of grassroots environmental groups all over the world who work to help reverse the tide.*
*We know that our business activity – from lighting stores to dyeing shirts – creates pollution as a by-product. So we work steadily to reduce those harms. We use recycled polyester in many of our clothes and only organic, rather than pesticide-intensive, cotton.*
*Staying true to our core values during thirty-plus years in business has helped us create a company we're proud to run and work for. And our focus on making the best products possible has brought us success in the marketplace.*

The **Meaningful Brands Index** measures the potential business benefits gained by a brand when it is seen to improve our wellbeing and quality of life. In 2016 it showed that:

- Meaningful brands gain, on average, 46% more share of wallet than less meaningful brands
- Meaningful brands see their marketing KPIs perform 100% better overall compared with less meaningful brand
- Meaningful brands outperform the stock market by 133%
- Trust is no longer enough: meaningfulness is the key driver for brand strength in an organic world

Charities should be the best organisations at explaining their purpose but in many cases companies are beating them to it. With this increasing trend, the ability of companies to invest money in telling great stories and the reduced trust in the charity sector, we run the risk of losing our place as the purposeful sector.

So why aren't charity brands making the same impact? After all, they exist to make the world better. The simple answer is that often charities forget to communicate their purpose. Instead they are so caught up in telling supporters what the organisation does and how, that they forget to communicate the reasons behind what they do. I often work with fundraising teams who are so focused on what they do and how they do it that they forget to keep articulating why they do it. The need is so obvious to us, working close to the cause, but it isn't always obvious to your donors.

## How is your organisation doing?
Could you, as a charity professional, describe your organisation's purpose in a sentence that makes people want to get involved? Try it now and see if it passes the simple, inspiring and memorable test.

Could you come up with a purpose for your team as well?

Now review your fundraising communications and see if you're focusing enough on the WHY.

How does your purpose factor into how your team and charity are run on a daily basis? Does it impact recruitment? Is it the deciding factor when you're making difficult decisions? Do you collaborate with other charities to have a shared purpose?

Let's reclaim purpose and use it to engage our supporters and teams.

Kath Abrahams of Diabetes UK on how important purpose and vision are for fundraising…

*"We're just developing a vision and mission for the charity. We don't have one that we see as an absolutely critical part of what we do. We want to articulate very clearly - this is our overall purpose and this is where we're headed. If you can hang everything from that, then it makes it much more understandable.*

*We've already got a solid strategy which I'm absolutely sure contains the right things. Then we can look at that again in the context of the overall purpose and direction of travel, and the fact that diabetes is so relevant right now. If that's true, than how do we maximize the opportunity that we have to make the greatest possible difference to people affected by the cause?"*

## Further reading
"Start with Why" by Simon Sinek or watch some of his TED talks

# NETWORKING

Networking. It's part of the job description, certainly at Director level and usually if you're heading up an income stream too. The word 'networking' conjures up images of dull conference rooms, strangers that you've got no interest in talking to, business cards and horrible wine. It's no wonder that many us of shudder when we hear the words 'networking events'.

And yet, I am a massive fan of networking. Because at its heart networking is about relationships. It's about friendships. It's about helping people. It opens doors to new opportunities. It's about learning and sharing. It expands my world beyond who and what I already know. And what's not to love about all of that?

So if the word networking has negative connotations for you then replace it with relationship building, or making new friends. Feel better about it now?

There are many articles on networking so I'm not going to try and teach you how to do it. I'm just going to share what I've learnt about how to make networking (in the sector and beyond) work for me and what I've gained from it. My aim? To inspire you to make this year the year that you expand your network and you love it.

**Find the situations that work best for you**
I've made new friends in all sorts of places – at meetings, on work courses, on holiday, online and at events. A room full of lots of people makes me wants to run away (truly) so I try and find, or create, more structured opportunities to meet people. For example - I found backpacking hard because I had to introduce myself to new people in each hostel, which is hell for a shy person. But I loved a backpacking tour where 30 of us travelled around Italy together and I made friends for life on that trip.

When it comes to networking, a structured event makes things so much easier. If the situation calls for you to talk to other people (as opposed to randomly going up to people) then that first tricky step is done for you. You're not interrupting anyone – you're just doing what is expected of you. After that you're just being friendly and interested in other people and that's easy, especially for fundraisers. So courses and events with workshop elements are a great way to build your network.

I also choose situations that bring out the best in me. Socially I'm shy but in a professional context I am confident so I know that I am comfortable in situations that have activities or involve talking about work. Parties are intimidating but a room full of Fundraising Directors or a workshop on leadership – much easier! For other people it might be the other way around – find out what works for you and focus on that.

**My top tips for networking events**

- I choose events that I'm interested in – usually with a speaker. Why?
    - I'm learning something - so even if I don't meet anyone interesting I've had a productive time
    - There's a built-in conversation starter - "What did you think of the talk?" or "Have you heard them speak before/read their book?"
    - I'm sat next to at least one person. Always say hello when you sit down and don't leave a gap between seats. It is so much easier to say "hello" the person sat next you than it is to approach a group of people in a room.
- I look for someone else on their own and go and say hi to them. They're often relieved, as nobody likes standing alone at an event.
- I have a couple of small talk conversation starters – then I'm not trying to think of something to say. They might be about the room, or the topic or the biscuits!
- I welcome other people to the conversation so that nobody feels left out.
- I look for people who look like they'd be potential friends. I want to have enjoyable conversations and that is more likely with someone who looks friendly and smiley.
- If I don't really want to go I'll take someone with me or arrange to meet someone there. We'll still mingle but it makes sure I actually go instead of coming up with an excuse.

**Be yourself**
As a fundraiser it is likely that you are naturally friendly, curious about people and helpful. Awesome – you're a natural networker.

People notice your energy. That may sound hippy dippy but happy, positive, friendly people draw others towards them before they've even started talking. We instantly like them. Before I go into a situation where I am meeting new people I take the time to leave behind the stresses of the day and I decide to be open, approachable and friendly. That changes my body language, my attitude and the general energy or vibe that I'm giving off to people.

The most interesting, inspiring and attractive people I know are really authentic. They know who they are and they like who they are and they don't edit it for other people. Give yourself permission to be authentic when you're meeting new people. If you're a storyteller and like being centre of attention then embrace that, equally if you're more interested in learning about other people and asking questions that's great too.

**Make new friends**
I resolved many years ago that when I went to a networking event my aim was to have a couple of good conversations rather than lots of dull ones. Genuine connections are hugely valuable, much more valuable than coming away with a handful of business cards. It also makes it so much less painful when your goal is to meet nice people. If I meet someone who would be useful for my business but whose company I don't enjoy, then I rarely stay in touch. I might connect to them on LinkedIn but that's about it.

These days I proactively reach out to people I'm interested in chatting to further and I have found people to be really open to that. I don't meet people that I have a genuine connection with every day, so when I do, I take the initiative and arrange to see them again. I've had one-off meetings with people and thought they were great so arranged coffee with them – they're now good friends. I've spoken on panels with people who have then hired me to facilitate a strategy day. Years ago, I saw the Institute of Fundraising was running a course for career changers and I thought that, as a fundraiser and career coach, I could contribute to that - so I asked if they needed a speaker. I was invited to speak on the panel and ended up meeting two great people. One has turned out to be a friend and my major donor guru and the other became a Trustee of the charity I was leading and then later gave me a job.

Those are just a couple of examples. Some of my favourite people are those I have met randomly at events or those I proactively reached out to. I saw a coach working with a client I really wanted to work with so I emailed him and suggested coffee. We now meet every two months for some of the most productive and thought provoking conversations I have.

I would really encourage you to listen to that little voice that says "I should speak at that event", or "I'd love to chat to that person more" and step outside of your comfort zone and reach out. The worse that can happen is that they ignore or politely say they're too busy. No harm done.

**Be helpful**
I never approach any relationship focused on what I can get from it. My first thought is always 'how can I help this person'. I'm always giving career advice, giving input on marketing plans and business models or suggesting a book, website or connection. I love to use what I know to help others and that has proved really useful in my career and business. I also love to learn. If someone runs a business I'm fascinated by the story behind it, the business model and what they've learnt along the way.

I often ask people what they need at the moment so that I can keep my radar on for it. As a former recruiter I'm always keeping my eye out for job opportunities for candidates who became friends. I keep an eye out for Trustees for my clients or business introductions I can make for people in my network. I do that because I love doing it but it also makes me a really valuable connection to have. If you're in my network and we like each other than I will be as helpful as I can be and as my earlier examples show, that helpfulness is reciprocated, albeit with no obligation or expectation.

I get asked for coffee to 'pick my brains' at least once a week now and sadly I can't say yes to everyone and still get my work done. But if a friend asks me to chat to someone who is important to them, I make the time.

I'd really recommend that you think about what you can offer other people when you network. I have a friend who loves to travel and always has a hotel or restaurant recommendation for her contacts when they're going on holiday and people think really fondly of her. You might be an amazing corporate fundraiser or great with spreadsheets. Whatever it is look for opportunities to help people. Did you have a great connection with that person? Did you notice they tweeted a question and you have an answer for them? Do you have some skills, knowledge or experience that is relevant to them that you could offer in return?

**Draw people to you**
The other aspect of networking is 'pull marketing' i.e. do things that draw people towards you, especially the people that you want to meet.

You could attend an event and meet a few people. Or you could be a speaker at an event and hundreds of people will know who you are and hear your message. Which one is the best use of your time?

Why just attend an IOF Special Interest Group when you could sit on the committee and build strong relationships with your peers whilst giving back?

Why not share your experience on a blog or publish on LinkedIn Pulse? LinkedIn and broader social media are great ways to reach out to people.

You could even write a book and ask people you admire to share their knowledge with you and the wider sector! This book has taken me a year to create but it has opened many doors for me along the way, introduced me to some of my fundraising heroes, let me write about the topics I am passionate about and will hopefully help lots of people in the sector stepping up into leaderships roles.

### Networking and fundraising

My network has made me a better fundraiser. I have nearly 3,000 connections from the charity world on Linked In (thanks mainly to my time in recruitment) and when I'm stuck on something I can reach out and get help. I find that particularly helpful for legal and technical questions.

If I wanted to be inspired I could reach out to other Fundraising Directors and have a coffee or bring a group of us together to discuss a topic that we're all wrangling with. I know people who can mentor members of my team and if I need a consultant or trainer I know lots of amazing suppliers. When I'm an Interim Director and recruiting for my team there are hundreds of people who will share my post and recommend working for me. People tell me about job vacancies before they go live.

When I'm speaking to corporate supporters I understand more about their business model thanks to the network I've built up in the commercial world and my curiosity about marketing and business models. I've read books recommended by my network that I wouldn't otherwise have discovered and I apply that knowledge to my work. I don't think like a typical fundraiser because I've expanded my world beyond that and it helps me to stand out. I've had a lot of practice of meeting new people, making genuine connections and being interested in them without being intimidated which has been great for major donor work.

I hope this inspires you to find a way of networking that works for you and that you enjoy. And I hope you meet some great people this year as a result. Good luck with it.

# TRENDS - TRANSPARENCY & TECHNOLOGY

Innovation often means evolving and keeping pace with how the world around you is changing. Technology and transparency are amongst the biggest factors impacting upon fundraising at the moment.

**Technology**
There is no denying that technology is changing our daily lives and that it is doing so at a faster rate than ever before. Social media is an ever-present part of our lives. We can now buy things using our phones and even our watches and entire industries have been disrupted by business models made possible by technology such as Uber and the sharing economy business models. So how is that starting to impact upon fundraising?

For some charities, such as Teenage Cancer Trust with Stephen Sutton, social media has **put service users directly in touch with the public** to raise funds, making the cause much more personal and inspiring people to give and raise funds. How could you encourage and support your service users to share their stories on social media? There is some useful advice in the interview with Catherine Miles later in this book, which shares how Anthony Nolan support patients with raising funds and awareness.

**Online influencers** such as bloggers and vloggers are becoming much more influential. Brands are paying influencers to become brand ambassadors because they have such huge followings and high levels of trust. Charities are catching on too and Save The Children worked with leading gaming vlogger PewDiePie and raised over $630,000 a couple of years ago.

Contactless payments are on the rise with one in seven payments now made by contactless cards. We are now starting to see charities trial contactless collection tins and CRUK had contactless collections at 16 locations on World Cancer Day in 2016. My personal favourite use of contactless is the Blue Cross canine fundraisers who has contactless technology embedded into their jackets so you could 'pat to give'. Contactless giving has been dubbed '**tap to give**' and looks likely to grow in the coming years.

It is also possible, given the backlash around individual giving techniques in recent years that donors will embrace fundraising methods that allow them to give digitally in a **one off way**. Contactless giving could well benefit from that trend.

In the States, a Hillarymoji app was launched which meant you could send various Hillary **emjois** (the mind boggles) and also had a donate button.

*"Consumers are increasingly using visual media to communicate with friends and loved ones. As the use of emojis increases, brands have an opportunity to connect with consumers in a more personal way. Especially with the use of emojis being described as the fastest-growing form of language, brands that partake in this form of communication will be able to more effectively convey their message."*
Mintel 2016 Report

**Virtual reality** is starting to become more mainstream now as part of a general evolution from an *information economy* to an *experience economy*. Digital experiences are going to be increasingly popular and there will be opportunities for charities who can tap into that trend. Oxfam recently trialled virtual reality experiences to show people how their donations were being used.

## Transparency

Donors are increasingly asking for transparency and being drawn towards causes where they can see the impact that their money makes really clearly. Microfinance non-profit Kiva was the frontrunner in this area enabling donors to choose their microloan recipients but in recent years other new entrants have made transparency a key part of their offering to donors.

Charity:water is the biggest example of this, allowing donors to raise funds and then see the exact well that has been built through the use of advanced digital tracking. Pencils of Promise in the States do something similar for building schools in the developing world. Pencils of Promise monitor and evaluate every project they set up and have a 'data impact hub' that shows impact across a number of different measures. I've seen other charities in the States sharing the details of all of their grants by giving live access to a Google sheet that shows all of their transactions.

Charity:water and Pencils of Promise secure funding for their core costs through major donors and companies, and although that has been a challenging model for Charity:water at times it has no doubt grown their public facing fundraising. Whilst most charities have a constant struggle to secure unrestricted income, these charities are being set up with the individual donor in mind. It will be interesting to see how Charity:water fares in the UK (it launched here in 2016) and how it impacts upon other charities. They're also utilising virtual reality in their fundraising video at gala dinners so are worth watching as early adopters of new approaches.

**Curation** is a growing trend in this era of information overload and with so many great causes out there and everyone presenting their impact in a different way major donors are becoming increasingly drawn towards services which curate and rate charities for them. For example Epic Foundation "connects the world's leading philanthropists and corporations with outstanding organisations focused on youth wellbeing." They have a portfolio of charities, which they select as 'high impact' after a robust evaluation process. They then allow you to monitor your impact in both statistics and via mobile, web and video. The final thing they do well is to create a community and the ability for high net worth individuals to experience the works they are funding through global visits. Epic Foundation charges no fees to donors.

If you started from scratch with your fundraising and charity how would you do things differently? How would you better connect the donors to the cause? And how can you take some of those principles and apply them to what you do today?

# STORYTELLING

## How stories work
Stories have been used to transfer information for centuries, from visual stories on cave walls through to parables and television programmes. We use stories to make sense of our world, to influence others, to sell products and to build friendships. Research shows that stories use the whole brain, activating language, sensory, visual and motor areas within the brain.

Storytelling also connects people. Researchers at Princeton University carried out an experiment where a graduate student told a personal story about going to a prom to 11 other students. All 12 participants were connected to fMRI machines so that the researchers could watch their brain waves simultaneously. The experiment showed that the same parts of everyone's brain were activated at the same time.

When the speaker was telling an emotional part of the story, not only did the emotional part of her brain light up, so did the same area in the brains of the 11 listeners. The same happened with their frontal cortex areas. Not only were they temporarily connected, the storyteller could plant ideas, thoughts and emotions into the listeners brains.

Stories catch people's interest, they are memorable and they emotionally engage people. We should be using them all the time in fundraising!

## What makes a good story?
Many stories follow a simple story arc, articulated by American author Kurt Vonnegut. He called the first story shape "Man in a Hole" – somebody gets into trouble and then gets out of it again. The second story shape is called "Boy gets girl" and it starts with an ordinary person on an ordinary day and something good happening to that person. Then the person comes close to losing that good fortune and things turn around right before the end to create a happily ever after.

You'll know when you listen to stories that some of them don't sit right because they don't follow a pattern or structure that is familiar to you. I always come away frustrated from those films that leave you hanging as to how things turned out in the end.

### Here is a tip from "Talk like TED" by Carmine Gallo…
*"Introduce heroes and villains. Whether it's a movie or a novel, every story has a hero and a villain. A strong business presentation has the same cast of characters. A spokesperson reveals a challenge (villain) facing a business or industry. The protagonist (brand hero) rises to meet the challenge. Finally the townspeople (customers) are freed from the villain, the struggle is over, and everyone lives happily ever after. In some cases the villain can be an actual person or competitor, but tread carefully in these cases. Above all, make sure the hero – your product, your brand or your idea - comes in to save the day".*

Make your stories personal to you – authentic emotion and vulnerability are incredible engaging. And give your story a context (such as who, what, when, where, why or time and place) but keep it brief or your audience will be sat there wondering when the actual story is coming.

### Telling your organisation's stories
When we mention storytelling in the context in fundraising, the obvious place to start is case studies – the stories we tell that show how our service has transformed someone's life. And those are some of our most powerful stories, where the villain is hunger or homelessness or climate change and our organisation is the hero. But how good are we at telling those stories?

Take a look at your case studies and compare them to the storytelling arc outlined above – are you making the most of the full story arc?

I suspect that many of us focus more on the detail of our intervention in our case studies, rather than on the life of the beneficiary before and after. You can tell me factually that you placed a well in an African village and now everyone has clean water. Or you can tell me about the life of a girl who used to miss school to walk for hours carrying heavy water and who now, thanks to the well you put into her village, can be a child again and go to school to build a future for herself. To some of you that will sound obvious but go back and look at which of your case studies are less powerful then others and ask yourself how you can tell better stories.

You need to give someone a reason to care and make it relevant to them. Sometimes that can be really simple. As you may recall, the general public's interest in the refugee crisis peaked when that heart-breaking picture of the young child washed up on shore was shared with the world. That picture told a thousand words and made what had felt like a distant problem very close to home.

**In "DO Story – How to tell your story so the world listens" Bobette Buster talks about 'threshold moments'…**
*"Stories are always about transformation. Whether we know it or not, whatever the story we are telling, we are always sharing a 'threshold moment'. This means that we are at a crossroads in our life, a turning point, a fork in the road. This threshold is a call for us to wake up, or to rise to a challenge before us. Fundamentally, we are being called to change. To discover the courage to become our best selves. This moment is always 'elemental' – a kind of fire, a spark carrying us towards transformation."*

The author argues that this spark can be handed on to your audience. *"The number one question your audience is asking is – why should I care? The central desire of anyone listening to a story is that they want to be moved."*

Some of the most high profile charity leaders such as Scott Harrison of charity:water are masters at doing this. And some of the best fundraisers I have known personally are natural storytellers, whether they are formally telling a story about the charity on stage or using stories about themselves or the world to connect with donors.

### Thinking beyond case studies
One of the reasons that I love meeting with service users of any charity I work for, is that it allows me to create stories of my own. I am not a natural raconteur and tend to be short and sweet in my communication. Being super concise is not great for storytelling, which requires build up to make people care. But when I think of the story I am telling as a journey I went on, then it gets much easier for me and I have a structure to work with. I find it easy to articulate:

1. What I felt and thought about something
2. What happened to change my mind
3. How I think and feel now

I use that structure (or some variation of it) because I can remember it, because it feels authentic to me and because I can use it to align with people who currently think and feel how I felt and thought at the start of the story – so I am meeting them where they are.

For example, you can tell stories to **donors** about the assumptions you had about how people became homeless before you joined the organisations before that, about the people you've met and the stories they told, and finally what you now realise about homelessness. That way you are telling your own version of the story that your audience can relate to rather than just recounting other's stories.

There are other contexts where stories are relevant too. You can use stories from what you've done in previous jobs to convince your colleagues in other teams that taking your proposed approach is the best way forward. You and your team can create a shared story about the vision and purpose of your team. You can tell stories to your team of your mistakes and how you learnt from failure to create a culture where failure is not feared. You can tell a new manager who is struggling all about your first attempt at line managing someone difficult, how you handled it all wrong and what you've learnt from that.

You can use stories to overcome objections, inspire your team to take action and help people understand each other better. It such a useful technique for getting people aligned with your thinking.

**Standing out from the crowd**
We live in a time of information overload and it can be hard for your organisation's stories to stand out. Social media is a wonderful tool for sharing stories and also encouraging donors and service users to share their own stories. The small brands with personal stories and passions behind them get much greater engagement on Instagram and Twitter than the big corporate brands whose only stories are slick adverts. Having said that the John Lewis Christmas advert has become a Christmas story telling tradition of late so it can be done.

Support your beneficiaries who want to tell their own stories – Stephen Sutton and Teenage Cancer Trust is an amazing example of this and Catherine Miles shares some great advice on this in her interview later in this book. This approach empowers beneficiaries and their families and is memorable and engaging.

Watch out for fundraising stories that your donors are telling on social media – they may be starting the next Movember of Ice Bucket Challenge.

Pick a few stories and craft them well rather than using large amounts of unmemorable case studies or campaigns. A well-planned integrated campaign can make a much bigger impact than the same effort out into lots of different communications.

**Further reading…**
"Talk like TED" by Carmine Gallo
"DO Story – How to tell your story so the world listens" by Bobette Buster

# INNOVATION

The largest charities in the sector have had innovation teams for a few years now but for a lot of charities' innovation is talked about but never becomes a priority. And yet, with existing methods of fundraising coming under increasing scrutiny and restriction, we are getting a clear message from the media, and some of the public, that fundraising needs to evolve. And of course we need to raise more money for our great causes.

Fundraising hasn't changed much in the 18 years that I've worked in the sector. Back then we already had face-to-face fundraisers and telephone upgrades and were piling money into those areas to create huge growth in income. All the other income streams looked very similar to how they look now and "relationship fundraising" was as talked about then as it is now. As a sector I believe we look internally far too much. Our conferences are full of sector speakers with an occasional token corporate speaker and we aren't even very good at sharing learning between the arts, education and broader social sectors. Digital is transforming business models in the corporate world but charities in the UK are yet to use it to shake up how we relate to donors and connect them to our causes. And as soon as one charity introduces a fundraising concept everyone jumps on the bandwagon and duplicates it.

In short, we are ready for a change!

Innovation can be defined as either *"to make changes in something established, especially by introducing new methods, ideas, or products"* or *"to introduce something new"*.

Before you can innovate, you need make sure that you have a **culture** that can create, incubate and implement innovative ideas.

**Embracing risk and failure** is crucial but really hard for the charity sector to do because money is in short supply and has been entrusted to us by donors. It is difficult to innovate if the pressure is on for everything to work perfectly first time. It is key to get your manager on board so that you have the freedom to try things that might not work, within agreed boundaries of course.

One way to start innovating is to look for continuous improvements to the way you do things now. Dave Brailsford, former performance director of British Cycling and team manager at Team Sky, has led two of the world's most successful teams to consistent success. He puts it down in part to always looking for the "**marginal gains**" – the small tweaks that the data tells you make a big difference.

Encourage your team to come up with ideas of how you could do things better and to actively seek feedback from donors about how you relate to them. Some of the best innovations come from getting better at listening to the cues you are being given.

As Arianna Huffington, founder of the Huffington Post puts it *"Innovation is never seeing yourself as a finished product. It is understanding that you are always a work in progress. It is about disrupting your own operations and looking at how they can improve. You must be your own disruptor."*

Then take a **testing approach** to improvements and innovations, testing new ideas before investing lots of time and money in them and iterate as you go along. You can't just change things – you need robust ways of finding out if your new solution is better.

**Prioritise creativity** by making time for it and giving yourself and your team the space to create new ideas. There are plenty of exercises you can do to think more creatively and you can reward people for ideas and innovations.

As important as your internal culture is, **look outside** of your organisation and the sector to spot trends. It is really hard to create a new market for a product but when you pick up on an existing trend, then the wind is at your back. Creating a product or service that people are actually asking for, or which donors are experiencing in another sector has an increased likelihood of success. Make sure that you are reading market trend reports, following early adopters in fields that are relevant to your organisation's work and spotting new business models and marketing ideas by reading widely and then discuss with your team how some of the ideas might translate into your fundraising. Look backwards as well – trends go in cycles and retro is cool so look back to the 70's and 80s and see what inspiration lies there.

Then make sure you have a robust system for evaluating the potential of new ideas and how you test them and integrate them in your work.

Kath Abrahams of Diabetes UK talks about innovation…

*"I think innovation is a bit of a buzzword. In the same breath I'd say it's one of the most important things that an organisation can do, if it does it well. If we aren't constantly thinking about what we could do differently and better, than our existing sources of income will just dry up. I think you have to nurture that in an organisation.*

*Interestingly when I was at Breakthrough we didn't have an innovation team but I did a piece of work where we developed innovation champions. We did have somebody who was our innovation manager. Her role was to make sure that she was a catalyst, so that helped facilitate a process of innovation. I think in the case of Breakthrough actually we had lots and lots of good ideas but people didn't know where to channel them and how to get them off the ground.*

*Some of the process is around working out how you develop good ideas and how you make sure that people across the organisation can feed into that. How you channel them. How you test and learn things. How you take a little thing and do it and think, "Oh that works!" How'd you grow it? What's the investment? All of that. The nuts and bolts around innovation. Systemising it almost in a way that doesn't destroy the creativity but actually enables the creativity to happen."*

Jools Tait talks about how celebrity foundations evolved as a new concept at CRUK…

*"I always thought there was mileage in something like the Bobby Moore Fund, a celebrity that was high profile, who was loved by the nation and was naturally associated with Cancer Research UK because he died of bowel cancer. You marry the celebrity, the cause and the output.*

*The Bobby Moore Fund had already been going for a number of years, and after working with Bobby's widow Stephanie I then took that model to Lawrence Dallaglio. As a team we helped set up Lawrence's foundation, which is still going today and the model was that we worked in partnership with him, but with no investment from CRUK, apart from our expertise and resource. He selected a project to fund and his commitment was initially £2million over two years. I think we worked with him to raise over £4million pounds over the time period.*

*So the celebrity registers their own charity, we gave them the model, the fundraising tools, the expertise and some resource, but no financial investment. We basically created a new product to go out to market with and we took that to celebrities such as Seve Ballesteros,*

*Jenson Button, Gordon Ramsay and JLS."*

Here's Jools again on where the next innovation in fundraising is coming from…

*"When Movember first came and registered that was interesting, it was different, it was a movement. As was the ice bucket challenge and its use of technology but then everyone tried to get on the bandwagon and find an ice bucket challenge equivalent. What interests me is where the driver comes from. Do the drivers always have to come from the charities? Or actually should we be more aware of and supporting the population and individual and society drivers?"*

**Further reading…**
There is an excellent book by Lucy Gower called "The Innovation Workout" that I highly recommend you read if you want your team to be more innovative.

"Winners" by Alastair Campbell has some really interesting chapters that cover how some of the most successful leaders and teams in the world innovate

# DATA ANALYTICS

*This is a guest chapter written by Andrew Barton. Andrew is an independent fundraising and strategy consultant specialising in helping charities achieve peak performance. Andrew has over 10 years senior fundraising experience at leading brands - Oxfam and World Vision - and many years of Director-level experience in marketing, CRM and strategic planning at Abbey National.*

Before you turn the page, are any of these issues bothering you?

- I need to generate more income on a fixed budget and I don't know the best way to re-allocate my investments for next year
- I'm under pressure from the Trustees to deliver results from our investments in major donors. I need some facts and figures to show them that we are on track despite the fact that the revenue isn't there right now.
- My individual giving team are running multiple tests on a new supporter journey for regular givers. But how do I know that the improvement didn't happen for other reasons?
- I know that many of my supporters are online and on social media channels. How can I know whether these channels can deliver great returns for me?

If so, then read on. Data analytics can help.

## Dashboards

When you're driving your car, it is second nature to look at the dashboard to check your speed, especially when there's a speed camera coming up. It is second nature to check you've got sufficient fuel to get to your destination. And, maybe you pay attention to the rev counter to make sure that you're maximising fuel efficiency, and not going to burn the engine out.

Analytical dashboards serve the same purpose. They give you an at-a-glance view to tell you what's going on. They will help warn you of potential problems and help you run your operation more efficiently.

There are two types of dashboards that will be useful to you:
1. *The fundraising management dashboard*: telling you (at high level) how your various fundraising streams are performing
2. *The supporter analytics dashboard*: telling you which types of supporters are especially valuable, which campaign tests are working and should be rolled out, which combination of channels are working best to drive upselling campaigns etc.

**Top ten tips for thinking about data and data analysis:**
1. *You aren't going to get any reliable insight, unless the data being collected is accurate.* It's "garbage in, garbage out." So, find out the processes that are being used to get the data onto the customer database. Is the data being re-keyed so creating the potential for error? Are there any processes in place to de-duplicate customer records?

2. *Make sure your data collection is legal.* Make sure you have the right consents in place to gather the data. This is increasingly important given the adverse publicity that's out there for breaches. As a simple rule of thumb, if you are following the ICO's best practice, then you should be in good shape when the new General Data Protection Regulation (GDPR) kicks in during 2018. The key action to take now is to read the ICO's Direct Marketing guidance and then look out for the additional guidance that is going to be provided by the ICO working together with the Fundraising Regulator. If you don't get the Fundraising Regulator's newsletter, then sign up.

3. *You aren't going to get trustworthy insight, unless there are consistent definitions for data.* It doesn't sound interesting, but if you are a senior fundraiser, it's critical there are some agreed definitions of things like an "active supporter." These should be consistently agreed across channels and fundraising streams. If you are an Individual Giving Manager, it's crucial that your regular giving programme has defined what the various payment statuses are so that you can then measure the impact of processes. For example, an active regular giver where a payment status is "overdue" should trigger a saving process, and you need to be able to measure the number of regular givers where a payment is made after proactive contact to "save" the donor.

4. *You need to have decided what you are going to do with the data you collect:* in

some channels (especially online) there is a trade-off between the amount of data being collected and donation completion. Do you really need everything on your form? If not, cut it out. Can you design your supporter journeys to collect some data at a later stage? Likewise, some of your fundraisers will want to survey supporters. Surveys can be a great way of capturing attitudinal data. But if you are going to use the data to drive fundraising direct marketing activity, make sure you can append the survey data.

5. *You need to do controlled testing:* Hold back that curiosity that wants to test everything. You need to A/B test one thing at a time. When testing, work out how many responses you need to *prove significance* before you test. Think it through. Do you have a big enough pool of supporters to prove a test given likely response rates? You can check this out beforehand by going online to find a significance calculator.

6. *Start small and build experience:* Don't try to run before you can walk. Build expertise. Ideally have a database manager and or data analyst in the team if you can afford them. Don't just look for technical skills when recruiting. Find people who will be great communicators with the fundraising team, and who can grow analytical skills in the team.

7. *Look for free, easy-to-use (or at least low cost) tools:* CRM databases don't have to be expensive any longer. For example, Salesforce now offers a Non-Profit Starter Pack where the first ten user licenses are free. There are also a number of data analytics packages like R that are also free. The key is having at least one team member that knows how to use the tools proficiently.

8. *Focus on value metrics, not vanity metrics:* there is plenty of data that is T.B.U (True but Useless) when it comes to driving the financial contribution from your fundraising programme. This is especially true of some digital measures. If you are a senior fundraiser in an organisation with a separate communications function, you may find the communicators focused on measures that assess reach. Number of Facebook likes, number of website visits etc. From a fundraising perspective, these are vanity metrics. They are a poor proxy for how much revenue you are going to drive. Your key digital value metrics are focused on response and conversion: how many visits on the donation page, conversion rate and average gift.

9. *Think about timescales when drawing up your fundraising management dashboard:* if you want to avoid being on the annual budget "hamster wheel" this is important. Some fundraising activities (eg a single gift appeal or an event) will generate costs and revenues in a one year period. Other activities (eg cultivating new major givers) will take longer. This is also true within fundraising streams. Take individual giving as an example- the revenue from a new regular giver from a Face to Face channel in year 1 will be typically 1.2 - 1.4 times that of a new single giver. But by the end of year 4, they will be worth 2.5 times as much. So make sure the key performance indicators (KPIs) for the longer term activities reflect things that are measurable <u>within</u> the annual budget cycle (e.g. the number of prospects at different stages within the cultivation cycle for major donors, or key predictors of future regular giving revenue like early attrition rates)

10. *Think about drivers of financial value when drawing up your fundraising management dashboard:* You want a dashboard that gives you early warning indicators, rather than telling you what just happened. For example, on a regular giving programme, the size of the initial gift is (in most cases) the single biggest driver of long term value, followed by attrition of donors after first, second and third payments. Make sure your dashboard is picking up these early warning indicators.

# LEADERSHIP INTERVIEWS

# LEADERSHIP INTERVIEW WITH ALAN GOSSCHALK

I interviewed Alan in early 2016 when he was Director of Fundraising at Scope. Widely recognised as a leader in fundraising, Alan has led some of most successful fundraising teams in the sector.

**How did you get into working in Fundraising?**
I did a French & Management studies degree, started doing accountancy exams, got part qualified and then decided I didn't want to do finance! I went into brand management at a food multinational and did a year there and loved it, but working for the world's biggest food company, you can't make much of a difference as a junior, and also it was obviously commercial and profit-orientated.

Then by chance I saw an advert in The Guardian for a job at Help the Aged on the database side and went for it and got it. That was in 1989. Help the Aged was at the time very strong in direct marketing and they invested and tested quite a lot. I spent 5 years there and became the head of department. From there I moved to Imperial Cancer Research Fund (as it was then, now it's CRUK of course) heading up all of their direct marketing and legacy marketing. I became a Fundraising Director at RNID (now Action on Hearing Loss) in 1997 and I have been a Fundraising Director ever since, at charities including Shelter and Scope.

So whilst working in the charity sector wasn't planned, once I came into the sector I really liked the people who were in it and the buzz it gave me. I was given quite a lot of responsibility, you obviously feel as though you are doing some good, and now I can't imagine being anywhere else really.

**How is your team structured at Scope?**
We have 45 people in our team and there are four team heads: Individual Giving; Events; Corporate & Major Donors; and Trust & Statutory. Quite

traditional. Our annual income is £22m this year, up from the £15m it was when I arrived here. That growth has come primarily from Individual Giving because we've been investing in recruiting lower level regular givers but obviously that growth is now significantly at risk. The likelihood is regulation will hinder growth or even reduce income, and I guess the question is, will that have a minor or major impact?

**How do you keep your team motivated in an environment that, at the moment, is a little bit hostile?**
We haven't become obsessed about the negativity, which it would be easy to do, because I think that could be very depressing. The team are motivated by their targets and what they achieve, and a strong team spirit for me has always been really, really important. Here, there are 45 people all on this floor, so it's quite easy to develop a strong team ethos, whereas if you're a charity with 300 regional fundraisers, say, that's a bit harder. I've always done a lot on the social side and on celebrating success, for example. We have 'Fundraiser of the Month' here and you can nominate your colleagues for going above and beyond in their job or putting some of the five Scope behaviours into action. The winner gets a £10 M&S voucher and a little cup to put on their desk for the month and people absolutely love it. Those sorts of things are really important in getting people to feel like they are a team with a communal aim.

Just because we work for a charity does not mean that we can presume that simply working here is enough to ensure passion and commitment. We also have an initiative that we call 'getting closer to the cause'. Service managers come in to talk and we go out to projects. We make sure people watch relevant films about the work and so on. It's not just up to individuals to do this as it's not going to be their top priority and it could fall by the wayside. We have activities in team meetings too so that people can learn about the impact of the organisation in a number of different ways.

**How do you develop and retain your fundraisers?**
I've really encouraged people to either try to get promoted internally or to consider being seconded, both within Fundraising and to other areas. For example, recently three fundraisers have gone into External Affairs. There's quite an active push to recruit internally, thus retaining knowledge and keeping staff longer than the stay of the average fundraiser.

As in many Fundraising teams, we still have quite big gaps in experience and knowledge between the Fundraising Director, the Heads of income streams and the level below the Heads. There's more movement in more junior roles, but it's quite a step up to be a Head, and then it's quite a step up to be a Director. I don't think we've cracked that.

## How would you define a successful Fundraising team?
I think they need to be always taking decisions based on what's in the best interest of the charity with respect to the supporters, working as a team and not be too insular in terms of who they're approaching and how. Seeing supporters as people in the round is vital. Relationship development is really important, both internally and externally, and good teams ensure that they're going the extra mile. Ultimately we want to be people's favourite charity so what is it that we can do to make them feel special about Scope and what Scope achieves, the information they're getting, and how they're engaged?

## How do you model that as a Fundraising Director?
I'm really clear that unless status is important to the supporter then you should be 'matching' the best person to engage with them rather than saying "I am the Fundraising Director so I've got to be matched to the director of CSR." Pushing people to try new things and saying it's okay to fail within reason is a good thing.

I talk about 'surprise and delight' quite a lot, about supporters and what they receive and how we communicate with them. It's about picking some things and being consistent about them with the people directly below you and then also when you're together as a whole team.

## How often do you bring your whole team together?
Every two months, we meet formally for a couple of hours but then we also do Fundraiser of the Month and when there are successes between times, we get people together. We have a thing called 'Fish' (which I didn't invent!) and when there are successes, someone sends around a 'Fish' email. It comes from one of the markets in New York where they chuck these fish at each other (!) and so when people have successes, they'll email round about those sorts of things. Some teams will do different things, so the Events team has got a 'success chain' that is a running email that they just add to when they get great feedback from people and to share other successes.

Obviously we want people within specific teams to support each other, and they're likely to be closest to each other – as opposed to people in other teams - but then also we get people socializing together to feel like a whole Fundraising division. There's a softball team, which is mostly made up of Fundraising and External Affairs staff.

I also organize a work-choir, and there's a concrete garden up here and some people have formed a gardening club. There's a cocktail club that people go to about once a month. There are quite a lot of fun and different things that people can engage in. Work needs to include some fun. People work pretty hard and are under pressure and so having some fun is a vital release.

**What lessons have you learnt about leadership?**
I would say that my ethos now is that some things are really important to get perfect. Like everyone, I hate things going out with typos on, but what are the big things to care about? I ensure that I am not critical unnecessarily – that would be very demotivating - and so it's mostly about being supportive and feeding in when I think something needs a steer. Even if something's not exactly how I would do it, if it's okay, then that's fine. People are different. I think there's a tendency when you're young to think that everything has to be the way you want it to be, and actually as you mature you realize that there are different ways of doing things and that people do a lot better when you're supportive of them and positive about them.

**What advice would you give to someone who is heading up an income stream and is looking to become a Fundraising Director?**
There are several elements to the job obviously. There is line management and fundraising capability to start with. Gravitas and credibility are important, but another key element is that as a Director, you've got to be valuable to the organisation beyond having your fundraising hat on. I think it's about getting involved in other areas where you can, and improving your strategic importance and your understanding of the rest of the organisation, because it should be a given that you're a good fundraiser if you're a Head of department.

Leading a 'directorate' is a bit different. You need to step out of being knee deep in the fundraising detail. Obviously, you've probably got a specialism in a Fundraising area and potentially a tendency to get most involved in that area, and that may not be the best thing for the organisation.

Being a Director is a lot more about managing upwards and sideways than managing downwards because you can control your area, but then you're the person responsible for listening to and influencing the other areas so that Fundraising can prosper. You're under pressure probably to increase your targets each year. The Chief Executive may or may not understand fundraising well, and then you've got a Board to work with and things will come in from left field at times, so I think you've got to be quite flexible and aware.

I spend quite a lot of time trying to sort things out that are issues for my Heads with other parts of the organisation, and trying to establish clarity around what is and isn't agreed, what can we fundraise for, when should I be getting involved and when not. I think I've got on well with the CEOs that I've reported to and they've been very supportive of fundraising so that does make life easier.

I also think that the Director's got a big role to play to role model the culture and behaviours that you want. You hear quite often of a change in leadership and someone being very different, and that having a massive effect on people and turnover. Good fundraisers are in short supply and they can move on very easily. I think you need to work hard at keeping people and generally I don't think all charities are great at that.

# LEADERSHIP INTERVIEW WITH CATHERINE MILES

When I asked fundraising colleagues which leaders they admired, Catherine was mentioned frequently, and with good reason. Currently Director of Fundraising & Engagement at Breast Cancer Now, I interviewed Catherine in early 2016 as she was leaving her role as Fundraising Director at Anthony Nolan and I found her approach to relationship fundraising inspiring and innovative so I'm really pleased to be able to share the interview with you here.

**How did you get into fundraising?**
I suppose I'm a career fundraiser since I've been doing it for 20 years. I was interested in fundraising after university because I'm very much focused on seeing the difference that I make, and as I soon as I fell into it like most fundraisers do, I thought "This is great, this is what I really like."

I was particularly interested in the major gifts side, which has become a theme of what I've done as a Fundraising Director. When I decided I was ready to move up to Fundraising Director level and started to look for jobs I was particularly keen on fundraising for charities where people have a personal connection to the cause. I was very interested in whether I could apply major donor theory to all areas of fundraising i.e. relationships with all supporters, whether those supporters were recruited by mass channels or individually.

Obviously, lots of people are very passionate about lots of different causes, but some of the strongest connections in the sector are in health charities, and of course Anthony Nolan supporters have a particularly strong connection to our cause because we play a direct role in people's treatment. We actually find you the stem cell donor that saves your life.

I was very interested in how you can take a charity that's got a fantastic case for support, but is raising less money than it should. A charity that certainly seems to have loads of potential, and loads of passion and enthusiasm and commitment amongst the supporters it has, but perhaps isn't fully harnessing that. And how can you actually have proper relationships with those supporters? How can you really understand what their motivations are, really talk to them about how they want to give money to the charity, or how they want to fundraise, and also all the other different non-financial ways they want to support?

That classic meta data approach of not looking at people in silos, not looking at people as cost centres, but actually thinking, "What is this person interested in, how might they like to help us, and how do we facilitate that, whether that's volunteering or campaigning, or awareness raising as well as giving and raising money?" I was very interested to see if you could actually put that into practice, or if it all becomes too difficult.

### Was your remit at Anthony Nolan to create change?

When I joined Anthony Nolan quite a few directors started at the same time and there was a new Chief Exec, and the mandate from the board very much "We really want this organisation to grow and develop, and we are open to hearing about how we could change" so it was great to have that sort of support from the Trustees. In the last 7 years we've changed pretty much everything in the fundraising programme.

### What was it like at Anthony Nolan when you started?

We were raising £4.6 million and £1.8 million net. It was very heavily dependent on events, with 60% of the money coming from some type of event. We had over 100 Anthony Nolan-owned events, zip slides and abseils, that kind of thing. We had quite a traditionally structured community fundraising team and no individual giving at all. Very low levels of legacy income. A little bit of corporate income but very much focused around a small number of big partnerships, not a broad base. Not really much to speak of in terms of the trust programme and no major gifts programme.

Essentially what we've done is grow all of the income streams, but in particular grown individual giving from scratch, which has provided 50% of our growth. Overall our total income this year will be £11.6 million, and £6 million net, so we've more than tripled net income.

### Wow. Well done. Are you exhausted?

Surprisingly, no! It's been fantastic, and we've been able to grow that at the same time as really investing in the charity's future - two things which are often difficult to do at the same time. Particularly when you're looking to build an individual giving programme from scratch, as we were from 2010 onwards. It was a period of time when that market was very mature and it was quite difficult for a new charity coming into that. You've got to carry several years of investment, so it was a question of me really understanding what the organisation needed in terms of how its finances worked. Not only the fact that the organisation, like all charities, needed more money and quickly, but really trying to understand actually what type of money the organisation needed from the fundraising team. Making sure that the fundraising strategy was synced to the organisational strategy, as they can often get a little bit decoupled and detached.

It was really important that the fundraising income was as secure and sustainable as possible, and also that a high proportion of it was unrestricted, and of course we had this huge dependence on events, which meant that the fundraising income could fluctuate a lot in a year. So we needed to try and invest in a base of regular givers to give the charity that diversity of income streams and provide that predictable income moving forward. Understandably, the Trustees were cautious on both reputational and financial grounds, so we spent a lot of time explaining – "This is what we understand about how the charity's finances operate, this is what the charity wants to do in future, this is the type of money it's going to need. If we're going to be able to do this sustainably and really have growing voluntary income that underpins the charity and doesn't fluctuate wildly year on year, we really do need to try and invest in individual giving." Then we had, and continue to have, fantastic support from the Trustees.

## How did you get Trustees on board for that investment?

I think it probably helped that quite a lot of them are accountants, actually. They've always interrogated the numbers in great detail and scrutinised us incredibly closely, which is absolutely right. It means they really understand what we're trying to achieve, in particular what we're trying to achieve in individual giving programme and how it's performing at any given time. They can probably tell you about as much of our individual giving programme as I can. It's great to genuinely have that partnership.

Of course it's particularly helped recently, because when the negative press coverage came, I think they felt well-informed about what we were doing, how we were doing it, and why we were doing it. Their scrutiny is far beyond anything that is being discussed now within the sector, and I think it's been beneficial, both for them and us as a fundraising team. We then built the individual giving base from scratch up to about 50,000 regular givers, but at the same time we also tried to grow all of the other income streams, so really building up the trust and major gifts programme, and that now gives us between £800-900,000 p.a and will hopefully continue to grow.

**Tell me about your approach to community fundraising…**
What we've tried to do is essentially implement major donor fundraising with community sources. I always had this theory that people generally in your community program are classic worker bees. They're people who proactively come to the charity and say, "I want to do some fundraising for you", and generally they've got a pretty good idea about what they want to do. They tend to be people who are very sociable, very energetic, and the sort of people who make things happen. I think we all know this, but somehow the charity sector started to view those people as providers of unsolicited cash. "These people will just do these things, we'll give them a fundraising pack, and they'll do all their bake sales, and we can just let them do that and then thank them for the donation."

What I felt was there was something much, much stronger and much more exciting there. That actually if you were energised enough to get onto a website or pick up a phone and say to the charity, "I want to raise money for you," you probably had a personal reason for doing it and the drive to make it happen, and I always felt there was probably an enormous amount of untapped passion and commitment and enthusiasm about those people.

Essentially what we did was restructure our community fundraising programme from the regional fundraising managers who were based all around the country. We centralised, that in two moves. We did one restructure and then another restructure and we have a team of relationship managers in London covering supporters across the UK.

They don't have any products, they don't divide their portfolio of supporters that they work with by type of activity. You don't have a fundraiser working on schools for example. They divide them based on financial potential - so exactly like a major donor programme would. When people get in touch with us that first phone call is absolutely key. We essentially ask them coaching questions about what's motivating them to support us, what sort of fundraising do they enjoy doing, who have they got who might be able to help them with the fundraising and who are they connected to?

All this amazing stuff comes out about why people want to raise money for us, and we enable people to realise they can raise more money than they ever thought possible. It's amazing what opportunities people have access to that they don't realise. We have very close relationships with them, do a lot of the classic type of major donor cultivation work and support them all the way through their fundraising, but also whatever else that they're interested in doing, whether that's awareness raising or volunteering.

What we find is of course that people are raising phenomenally more than they would do otherwise, and interestingly they're going out and getting other people involved, so they're almost running mini local fundraising campaigns. So there's this massive cross-feeding of all the programs, because they're essentially acting as like ambassadors, which is fantastic.

We've had more than ten £100,000 plus relationships and something over 50% of the net income comes from the top 50 supporters, so we're essentially getting fundraising campaigns that are actually at major gift level. And they go on and support us year on year and they are great news advocates for us, doing press and PR. There's a very interesting cycle you sometimes you see where they have a very intense burst of fundraising, then they go through a period where perhaps they're doing some volunteering for the charity, and then a couple years later they come back to fundraising again. It's pure relationship fundraising basically. It's about having those multifaceted relationships. That's very interesting, and it's because we're not trying to silo them, and also we're not trying to force them down a particular activity, whereas I think a lot of charities where their community fundraising programme is very product-based, if somebody gets in touch with them, I think there's a natural inclination to say "Do our cake sale at work in December".

**How does that impact on your recruitment, because I suppose for that team you're not looking necessarily for traditional community fundraisers?**
It's difficult. Conventional community fundraisers often don't have the experience of working this way, so we've either had to find people that have got a major donor background or train and promote people internally. People joining us at the more junior level have been promoted very rapidly, because it's all about your personal attributes as a fundraiser. Can you listen well? Can you build rapport? Can you understand the cues that you're getting from the supporter, and can you suggest something really relevant for them to do? Those fundraisers have to be able to talk about anything that the organisation does, or any way that a supporter could help us - which means that they actually develop far quicker and it makes for an interesting job.

It also means that we have to work very cohesively across the organisation and across the fundraising division. Particularly when we have patient appeals, which is when someone (typically a child) urgently needs to find a stem cell donor, and a family will contact us, and there will be a very, very intensive period of public awareness. It'll often be very driven by social media, and it's very much the family leading those appeals. Those can either have very intensive bursts of publicity, or people joining the stem cell register, or people raising money, or people doing a combination of all 3. What we have there is very sort of loose and flexible - like little project teams from across the organisation.

## How so you co-ordinate those appeals – presumably it involves quite a lot of people?

We have a patient appeals summit and that involves all of the people across the organisation who might be touchpoints for patient appeals. So our patient support teams, our donor recruitment staff in the field who sign up the stem cell donors, right through to our press team, and our social media team - because of course often the first time you spot things is when something just pops up on Twitter, and you have to respond very fast. We try to understand a bit about what are the families going through, where they are in that transplant journey, and then we work out the best way for us as an organisation to support them. There's always one main point of contact with the family, which tends to be the team where the family arrived in the organisation first and then behind that, there's always this loose group of representatives from all the relevant teams that are involved.

You can imagine how many press enquiries can come hurtling in to the family and one of the things we try to do for them is help field those press enquiries, because it can become a huge news story very, very quickly. The media pressure can be very intense and these people are in the middle of an incredibly traumatic period of their lives. We've learnt with some of the very, very big ones how quickly we need to respond, how closely we need to coordinate internally, so usually during those periods, little project team will meet every day even if only quickly. Then over time things will calm down.

It's amazing what people can achieve for charities in a very, very short period of time in those situations. They can make a massive difference to a cause and they can build these extraordinary social media audiences. I think there's a really interesting journey that the patients and their families at the heart of those stories go through. It can be exhilarating and uplifting, and they can feel a huge amount of public support, but then the flip side of that is you've also got the public scrutiny at an incredibly traumatic time, and of course you can also get your 1% of the population who starts behaving like trolls on social media. Our role is to support people as much as possible.

I think there's a very interesting thing for charities working with those patients around always making sure, which I think Teenage Cancer did incredibly well with Stephen Sutton and his family, that the appeal is actually being owned and driven by the patient and their families themselves. Even if there are opportunities coming up that would be big, high-profile ones, it's really, really important that the family feels in control, that they're driving, and that they're deciding what they do and what they don't do. I think sometimes some charities find that nuance difficult in the heat, and particularly where things move so fast with social media.

You can then build those relationships into long-term relationships that evolve into lots of different areas, but you've got to have those relationship building skills internally, and it is so important that the supporter is in control. Too many charities have either got themselves set up in the enormous mass fundraising style, or I think some fundraising teams have a bit of an urge to control rather than give supporters freedom and autonomy.

**Does this model scale?**
I hope so, I'm about to find out. I'm joining Breast Cancer Now as Fundraising Director, so I will let you know. I think obviously there are logistical advantages from the fact we're all in the same room, but essentially the model we have is that each relationship manager in the community team is looking out for about 200 people at any one time. Some of those relationships, exactly like a major donor programme, will be very active, others will be in the stewardship phase, others will be right at the start. So I think if you were in one of the very big charities that had a huge number of supporters with a personal link to the cause and keep those principles of a relationship manager with a portfolio of supporters they
are working with to build relationships and empower people to raise money in the way they want, I think it's absolutely scalable. I think all that happens is you've just got more people doing that with more supporters.

**How do you spot whether someone's going to be a good relationship manager? What are you looking for?**
People who are capable of building rapport with a wide range of people. Generally, the successful ones tend to be people who are very interested in other human beings, and can listen really well. They need to be able to listen, realise what the supporter is hinting that they might be interested in doing, and then correctly pick up on that cue and come back with a relevant suggestion. Some people can listen really well but what they can't do is pick

up the significance of the cue and suggest something relevant. That ability to listen and actually respond actually very quickly, all within the same face to face or telephone conversation is very important.

Then within that, we've got people with very different personalities, actually. We've got some people who are very bright and bubbly, very outgoing, and they build rapport just because they're so lively, and you just hear lots of laughter going on the phone with them. We have others who are quiet, a little more reserved, but incredibly caring and clearly really emotionally connect with the supporters, and they're just so sympathetic on the phone.

**When people are building personal relationships with someone who is at an emotional point in their life, how do you maintain those professional boundaries? Some of those relationships must edge into being personal relationships?**
We talk a lot about that, we do training around that and we have a lot of support from our patient experience team. Particularly training around how to handle relationships with people who are either a traumatic stage of their life or indeed have been recently bereaved, because obviously we have a lot of people who have been recently bereaved and immediately are calling us within a short number of weeks of their loved one dying, or we have ones with patient appeals where we actually work with the family all the way through. That can be incredibly hard for everyone here when you're working, particularly with a child patient, and they don't make it, and that's incredibly tough.

We offer a lot of ad hoc support - so the patient team are great if you've come off a difficult call, or if you've hit a period in the relationship that feels difficult or is making you question how to handle things.

We also talk a lot in fundraising about where that line is between building great relationships with people and understanding that there are boundaries, that you're still representing the charity, and that it still has to be a professional relationship, even if hopefully they do feel that they have a connection with you and they can trust you. Our supporters are at times telling us extraordinarily personal stuff and you're seeing them at absolutely the most traumatic time of their lives. There's a constant discussion, a lot of the time often between me and the head of that team with everyone where we try to talk about situations very openly, and we review what scenarios have come up and how have we handled them.

A lot of the time these fundraisers are very young. Some of the more senior fundraisers of that team are 23, and they're working on 6 figure relationships. Because they're good enough to do that, but they are young people who are frequently talking to parents who have just lost their child. We emphasise the fact that the relationship is a close and supportive one but it is a professional one, not a personal one, and you can't have things going into being a personal relationship.

We do a lot of in-house training. We train on everything from how you handle the first phone call, and the great coaching questions to ask supporters to really help them understand how they can raise money, all the way through to how to do assess people's potential.

There is also a lot of work on how the teams work together and the power of the network, which were currently doing huge amounts on. That's when you get into that really interesting thing of supporters going and getting other supporters, but to do that, you've actually got to have all of the fundraising teams working together, and you've got to have a completely commitment from all the fundraising teams that what's most important is the money that we're trying to raise for the patients we're trying to help the experience that we're giving the supporters - not our own individual cost centre codes.

For example, a supporter came in, he'd had two transplants, and they're celebrating his survival from his second transplant by doing a row down the River Thames because he'd been a rower, so the community was supporting him - fabulous, raised a whole lot of money. By chatting to him, it turns out, he's a director of a gym chain, and they've never had a charity partner, so that's panned out into a corporate partnerships which is fantastic. Now he's running the marathon for the sixth year and at the same time they had a big celebration party to celebrate his latest transplant anniversary, and that went so well they're thinking of doing that every year, so it's almost a bit like 6 degrees of separation reverse. We could've done a great job on that first relationship, but if the community team hadn't been thinking about what else this supporter could do it could have stopped there.

Even if people are supporting in ways that sit in lots of different cost centres, our database reports everything back to us about the whole campaign, so we can completely report back to supporters about the number of people are doing this event, this number of people who have given cash donations, and the grand total. We do that all the time because it's so important for them to know who's doing what and often people won't necessarily tell him straight up what they're doing. We haven't done particularly formal tribute funds so far, but we'd certainly be open to that.

We've got quite a lot of supporters who fundraise for restricted projects and that's absolutely fine.

**How do you retain your staff? You've given them a lot of experience very young and in a major donor approach too. Those candidates are like gold dust to recruiters and charities.**
We chain them to the desk ;). Our overall staff retention rate is somewhere between 2.5 and 3 years, so it's longer than I think the sector average overall for fundraisers.

It's a combination of factors. We invest in people's training and personal development, and we really encourage people to go out and speak and conferences and workshops and that sort of thing as part of their development. We support people through professional qualifications. We do a huge programme of in-house training that is continuous and we have the coaching staff, and the insight profiling, which is very much focused on them as individuals, and how do they work with others, how do they work best, where do they want to go in their career.

The fact that we work together so collaboratively means they're getting a lot of experience of a lot of different income streams. We do have a big track record of promoting people internally. We absolutely don't operate a closed shop, because I don't think that's helpful at all, and we always do open recruitment, but inevitably a lot of our junior fundraisers are getting a lot of really good, solid experience and when vacancies do come up, they often are really well positioned to go for them. For example at the moment, three of the five heads of fundraising were promoted up into those roles, and I think particularly when it reaches that level, it's sends very positive signals that you can not only go up to the junior levels, but you can also go up to head of team level.

Also, as you can imagine, it's an incredibly emotive charity to work for. The general working atmosphere across the charity is very good. People are very nice to one another. I think people have a very strong emotional commitment to the organisation, and it's incredibly tangible. It's the most tangible place I've worked as a fundraiser - we meet the patients every day who are alive because of what the charity does and the money we've raised, and that's hugely motivational too.

We have an overt emphasis on people's personal development and we're very open about the fact that we're investing in them for what they'll deliver here, but also equipping them for their future career that might be here or might be elsewhere, and that's okay. It's absolutely fine to have those conversations about where they want to go in their career very openly. I think that hopefully makes it an environment in which they feel like they're being invested in and they want to stay. A lot of fundraising teams I've worked in have had a very weird thing about not being open about that, or everything around learning and development being within either very narrow confines of which training course do you want to go on, or "is this definitely going to help your job right here and now?" Obviously it's important to do that, but it's also about developing the individuals more broadly, which will benefit us in the long run, because the more great fundraisers we're pumping out into the sector, in the long run the better for everybody.

# LEADERSHIP INTERVIEW WITH JENNI ANDERSON

I interviewed Jenni in early 2016 when she was Income Generation & Marketing Director at Haven House Children's Hospice based in Essex. That was her first Director level role and she's making a great impact at the charity. Her team were Finalists in the National Fundraising Awards 2015 - Fundraising Charity of the Year. Jenni is now Director of Fundraising at Duke of Edinburgh Award.

**What's your income at Haven House?**
Our turnover this year will be around £3 million. Like many hospices, we receive a small percentage of statutory income and for us it's about 23%. So overall, our fundraising income target for this year is £2.3 million.

**You've seen great growth in your time there I understand?**
I've been there three years this January and in that time we've doubled the income. It has been hard work, we've had four years of growth and that's been achieved because of the team we have there.

**So how did you, as a team, create that growth?**
Primarily, we've invested in people. Growing your income is of course about having good fundraising products and engaging your donors and supporters regularly with activities that are right for them. But it's also about having the right staff for you to be able to do that.

Many charities can find it difficult to justify the investment in people. If you want to have a sustainable organisation, then you need to have a diverse fundraising portfolio and that includes fundraisers. Wouldn't it be great if charities could employ two people in an office and be presented with a million pound legacy every year? Unfortunately that's not going to happen in reality. You have to have people doing the work, so that when those million pound legacies do come in, they're an added bonus, an incredible windfall.

## How did you identify where to put new staff and where has your growth come from?

What is lovely about the hospice sector is that we're very good at helping each other learn and develop. We're very good at sharing. Regardless of location, if you're looking for evidence of a particular idea, someone will say "I know somebody who's done that" and you can have an honest chat with them. When I started at Haven House, I did quite a lot of fact finding and the sector was very accommodating.

I do also like seeing how growth models and theories can be put into practice. One of my favourite models is Ansoff's Growth Matrix. You can always make improvements to your existing products in your existing markets but if you want to grow, you've often got to go in different direction. It also encourages you to look at your competitors to identify your gaps.

So we analysed what other hospices were doing, what sectors or activities they were working in and where they were seeing a good return.

As an example, Haven House joined a hospice lottery partnership in the months before I started. For the first year, we grew our player base and three years later, we're at 7,000 players. It isn't an innovative fundraising idea, but it was innovative for us at the time.

Retail was another growth area. We had one shop and our long-term plan is to open seven shops. We're now at four. We can use our shops to analyse our growth – for example does a shop impact positively on supporter growth? And we can see (using postcodes and the wonders of Google Maps) that it does.

Before we embarked on our shop expansion plans, I visited hospices and other charities that had 20 shops and asked, "When you were opening your 20 shops, what did you do?" It was important to our Trustees that we had done our research, as retail can be a huge financial risk for a charity. Learning from others helped us to develop our plan.

## Is managing a retail team different from managing traditional fundraisers?

I have a Head of Retail who manages our retail team. They are remote workers and this comes with challenges. Investing the time in visits is important, but we've only got four shops. If we had 20 shops, would that be a realistic thing to do as a Director of Fundraising? Probably not. Those staff, who are working incredibly hard, may then only see you once a year. As a Director who sees her team on a daily basis, that feels like an anathema to good team working.

**It sounds like you enjoy doing your research?**
Yes, I spent some time reviewing all the benchmarking reports for the sector, and went through it line-by-line comparing our performance. I would recommend this for anyone going into a new role, either at Director or Head of department level. It's still important to talk to people though. You don't just sit at desk with a few reports and then pull out your plan and say "This is what we're going to do."

There are still many things that other charities do, that I look at and think "We could so easily do that. How are we going to do that?" I try and encourage my team to look at what others are doing. If we're a £4 million charity and there are £10 million hospices out there, what are those £10 million pound hospices doing that we're not doing? How do we get there?

I am fortunate that I work in an organisation that is comfortable with fundraising. Some of the activities we've implemented are investment heavy, and we couldn't do it without the support of our colleagues and Trustees.

**You've seen a lot of growth over a short period of time. Is the plan to sustain that? What is your strategy going forward?**
Last year our senior team worked together with our Trustees on a new five year strategy – our first – a Vision for 2020. By 2020, we want to help 500 children. From a funding perspective this means we have to raise £5m, about £1.4m in additional funds. Which is a bit bold, isn't it, really, when you think about it?

**It's quite a lot for a team that's already performing well. I always find that if you go in somewhere new there's always room for improvement and that can give you some significant growth. But then how do you grow, when you've got a team that's already motivated and they know what they're doing. How are you going to go about doing that?**
The second piece of work that I did around the benchmarking was to look at the short, medium and long-term. The long-term pieces were to build the lottery and retail. The short-term was about refocusing people and teams. I have a great team, but when I started the accountability lines weren't that clear. Everyone did a bit of everything. For example fundraisers were presenting to school assemblies in the morning and then meeting a potential major donor in the afternoon.

So we redefined who was looking after what, and then plugged some gaps. The community team were doing really well with that audience, and to help them do even better we moved high value into a new team.

**What happens when someone says, "I used to raise this much, but then you took out the thing that raises me quite a lot of money, and now I've got to make up that income?" Did it come up and how did you tackle it if it did?**
It did come up. However, what we raise as a team – the bottom line - is more important. I am clear that our culture should not be about saying "That's mine". We set some values that say "This is how we're going to operate together; we're going to help each other out, we're going to let each other know when we're busy and we don't want to be disturbed, we're going to let each other know when we're a bit stressed". Sometimes some things are not going to work as well and others will and we'll celebrate those things together. More importantly it shouldn't matter to the children we're looking after what 'line' that income sits in. The focus should be on them.

**Where else is growth going to come from?**
The areas with the high ROI (return on investment). Grants and trusts, major gifts from individuals and major gifts from corporates. We now have a corporate and major gifts team, and our high-value events and our major gifts work together.

The only other piece of the puzzle, which I don't think small charities put enough investment is put into, is brand and marcomms. I think it goes hand-in-hand with raising money, finding volunteers or opening up your service to new beneficiaries. If you have a poor website, or you can't spell in your thank you letters, or you would never do a press release or you're scared of talking to journalists, then I can't see you engaging with those who could give you time or money.

Good marketing is also not about looking slick or spending lots of money on agencies. It is about being proud of your brand, and not letting it be used inappropriately. Coca Cola cares about their brand. Innocent Drinks cares about their brand. Why shouldn't you have the same view of your own brand? You should protect it and love it and think through who can use it.

**How do you find the right people for your team?**
Sometimes the hospice sector gets seen as the place to go if you want a "nice little job". If that comes across when we interview a candidate then they are not going to come and work here. All fundraising is quite hard.

Plus just because you've decided that you'd prefer to work closer to home it doesn't make you less of a professional fundraiser than someone who is trekking in to London every day. In short, recruitment is one of my biggest challenges.

It is also tough because when you work in a hospice, you see exactly where the funds are being spent. We see families come through the door, leave their children with us, and we also see families come through the door who don't go home with their children. You cannot work in that environment and think, "I'm going to go home at 5pm today." If you care, and that must translate to any cause you care about, you will always put in the extra effort, because you see that the money raised is being spent well, and you want it to make a difference.

**Any advice on the first 90 days as a Fundraising Director?**
First do an assessment; you look at where the gaps are, you look at the improvements that are already there, you look at what's going really well, and then you reflect on whether you need to make any changes or not. You are either the type of person who does that immediately, or, you maybe do it over six months to a year. Your personality will drive how you approach those things. I don't think there is a right way, and hopefully if you're going into a new job, you've been given a heads up about what they would like you to do, rather than you're just faced with the question "Is this a 'I've got to change this around really quickly' type job, or is this a 'this team is doing really well and we just want to grow by X percent each year' job? Hopefully you'll have been able to prepare for this in advance.

**What's your approach to management like?**
I feel fortunate every day. I work in an open plan office, so I see the majority of my team daily. I get involved in anything my team wants me to be involved in. I have always said "I know this is happening, do you want me there?" One of the things I learnt from another hospice fundraising director was to spend your first six months going to everything. So I did that. I went to everything. I went to school assemblies, I went to bucket collections, I went and worked in the shop, every networking event, every event coming up, I went to. Some of those, I had a job to do, and some of those, I just watched. Then after that, I said, "right, I'm not going to go to everything anymore, but if you need me (and it's the same for CEO) if you need us to be there, to perform a role that you can't do, we will do it. If you need us because you're desperate because someone's dropped out, we'll do that as well". I think last time we met I'd just done a bucket collection at Canary Wharf at 6:00 AM.

## How do you stay motivated?

Everyone has bad days, and things that don't pay off. You predominantly have to have a positive outlook on life, which then means that when you have setbacks and make mistakes, yourself as well as your team, you are not going to let that cloud everything else that you do.

## What was the most useful thing that you did before becoming a fundraising director that you really value now that you're a director?

One of the things that I've enjoyed doing is working in organisations where you're able to work cross-functionally, or with other teams, outside of your day job. If your job takes up a hundred percent of your time, then where are you going to develop? You're only ever going to develop in that particular function. To take the next step up, you need ten percent of your time to expose yourself to different activities or different parts of the business. For example, if you've never presented to a subcommittee of the board before, when you're in a director position, or even if you're a head of team, you will be expected to present to the board. Can you find a way to do that now to give you the experience and confidence needed for later in your career?

It is about taking that step up when the opportunity arises. If your boss is off, but there's a finance committee that week, could you go in their place? Even if you don't say anything, you may learn from the conversations around you. If you want to be in a position where you're managing a team or larger income streams, you are going to have to step out of your comfort zone. Building confidence is key so find ways to acquire the skills you will need and will subsequently build that confidence.

For example how would you write a business plan? Have you done some benchmarking? Have you looked at your competitors? Made an assessment of the pros and cons to taking forward an idea? You can only learn by doing it. So you give it a go, you present it, people ask you questions, they find holes in things you've written, and you improve it next time.

I would consider myself a professional fundraiser. By that, I mean, I've spent time educating myself and I've been lucky to have learnt from others inside and outside of the organisations I've worked in. If you just look inwardly, you're never going to develop.

I completed the MSc charities pathway at Cass Business School. I found that hugely beneficial. It's an MBA for the charity sector. It goes through all of the things that charities need to do to be sustainable. Governance, resources, HR, the whole gamut. It's a safe learning environment, where it's okay to ask stupid questions, it's okay to have debates, it's okay to be challenged back as well. I would recommend that.

**How important is networking to doing your job well?**
One of the things I know I need to do more of is just getting out there. I'll quite happily sit in front of the computer and read people's blogs. I do go to networking events, but I have to make myself go to them. If I'm going to a conference or drinks, then I'd like to get something out of that that I can take back for the hospice or for my team.

**One final question, which is, what's the best thing for you about leading a fundraising team?**
Going into work every day and working with a truly great bunch of people that care about the same things that you care about, and you know that they would be prepared to help you out if you needed it, and they know you're prepared to help them out. When you have to spend eight to ten hours a day of your life with people that you are not married to and are not family, and you didn't choose each other, you have to think that they care about you and you care about them.

# LEADERSHIP INTERVIEW WITH JOOLS TAIT

Jools Tait kindly agreed to be interviewed after being named as an inspiring leader and fundraiser by one of her former colleagues. Her impressive 14 year career at Cancer Research UK (and its predecessor Imperial Cancer Research Fund) included roles as Head of Special Events & The Bobby Moore Fund, Associate Director and Director of Corporate Partnerships & Celebrity Foundations.

In 2014 Jools moved to BEN (Motor and Allied Trades Benevolent Fund) as Director of Business Development and so she has a really interesting perspective having been a fundraising leader at two very different organisations.

**So how did you get into fundraising Jools?**
I got into fundraising in the States, after I left my career as a primary school teacher in the UK and in Milan. I'm a US citizen as well and when I moved to Boston I joined a charity called Walk for Hunger, which organised the largest annual, one-day fundraising event - 40,000 people in the state of Massachusetts. From there I did more event fundraising as well as undertaking fundraising consultancy for the American Cancer Society before I came back to the UK and joined Imperial Cancer Research Fund in 1997.

**And how did your role evolve at Imperial Cancer Research Fund and then Cancer Research UK over the years?**
I joined as a London Events Manager and organised all of the high-profile events in London. And then quickly took on some campaigns such as our Breast Cancer Awareness Month campaigns and then I coordinated national fundraising with all the regional teams.
It became clear that my speciality was in the high value space i.e. high-value events, high-value donors and building relationships and partnerships. That naturally took me into the bespoke niche fundraising streams like the Bobby Moore Fund, and big third party events and then I moved to

corporate fundraising and still kept high-profile niche with celebrity foundations.

**Celebrity foundations within charities were a new evolution at that point. How did that come about?**
I always thought there was mileage in something like the Bobby Moore Fund, a celebrity that was high profile, who was loved by the nation and was naturally associated with Cancer Research UK because he died of bowel cancer. You marry the celebrity, the cause and the output.

The Bobby Moore Fund had already been going for a number of years, and after working with Bobby's widow Stephanie I then took that model to Lawrence Dallaglio. As a team we helped set up Lawrence's foundation, which is still going today and the model was that we worked in partnership with him, but with no investment from CRUK, apart from our expertise and resource. He selected a project to fund and his commitment was initially £2million over two years. I think we worked with him to raise over £4million pounds over the time period.

So the celebrity registered their own charity, we gave them the model, the fundraising tools, the expertise and some resource, but no financial investment. We basically created a new product to go out to market with and we took that to celebrities such as Seve Ballesteros, Jenson Button, Gordon Ramsay and JLS.

**How interesting. What were the challenges you faced getting that new income stream to work successfully?**
The challenge was all about the relationship - how did you get to those individuals? How did you get through the management company to the decision makers? And how did you show them that this model would add value to their brand and give them a different profile in the marketplace?

We also picked those celebrities where CRUK as a brand didn't have a natural inroad. So "youth" was a big problem for us. They were turned off by CRUK. You know cancer was something old people got. Whereas, JLS could talk to their fan base on our behalf about healthy living and cancer prevention and that was appealing to both parties.

In corporate partnerships we were also slightly reinventing the traditional corporate model of the time. General philanthropy was on the out and our approach was really identifying what assets have we got that are attractive to each corporate partner. And we started with a fact-find. What are their objectives? What are the challenges they are facing? And how could we then go back and tailor a pitch, so they thought 'hmmm actually the problem is customer retention, or the problem is new customer base or the problem is this' and how could we partner with them to solve the problems.

So that was my journey through CRUK and I finished there in 2014, having done those years as Corporate and Foundations Director and I have more recently moved to a smaller charity, BEN, as their Business Development Director which is a whole new challenge, because it doesn't have the engine room that CRUK had. It isn't a household brand and it's not consumer-facing in its fundraising. It's niche by industry and there are different challenges there but the principles are the same.

**What do you think you learnt from your time at Cancer Research UK, in terms of fundraising and leading successful fundraising teams, that you could transfer across to BEN?**
The most important thing, I think to me, whether it was building a team or being successful externally, was building good relationships, having great communication skills. Because people buy from people whatever you're selling. It doesn't matter how great your brand is if you're a really difficult, non-communicative individual, they'll never engage with you. And then it's really, also understanding the power and the importance of those relationships and maintaining them and developing them. And not just - go in, make the sale and leave.

And building teams internally with different strengths. So within a fundraising team, actually having different skills and different strengths, but always considering cultural fit and
those interpersonal soft skills that no matter how hard you try, you can't teach people, to be good with people. People are either engaging or they're not.

**And how do you pick that up at interview? Because there are quite a few people who are good at playing the interview game, aren't they? And then they get into an organisation and actually the fit just isn't there at all.**
You also have a gut instinct feel of 'do you know what, they will really fit the team' or that they get the sales model. You see their enthusiasm. How they communicate. They're not robotic in how they've prepared for an interview. Also by asking at interviews more about them as an individual and the things they do outside work and what motivates them and where their hobbies lie. Rather than just career skills because they practiced that and mastered that to within an inch of its life.

You never go into a meeting and find it 100% what you expect it to be. You've got to be able to think on your feet and engage someone with the organisation, in any situation. An MD, a CEO or whoever is in the meeting, will throw a curveball so in an interview, if you throw those curveballs out, it's also quite interesting to see how people react in that situation.

And some people nail it and you know they've got the gift of the gab and can think on their feet.

**What was it that appealed about moving to a smaller organisation?**
I didn't want to go in and do the same thing with a different brand. And if you look at the other top ten, whether it's Oxfam, Save the Children, NSPCC, British Red Cross, Macmillan I can picture their org charts. I can picture their hierarchical structure. I can picture the departments and how it will work. And there's a lot more political, operational hoops, hurdles, processes to get through and you sort of have to prove in some ways your credibility to make some quite big changes. Whereas, going into a smaller organisation, do you know what, they are so excited, from the Board of Trustees to the Chief Exec, to have somebody that thinks a little bit differently.

The big charities are 100% about the bottom line. Nothing else matters and that's where a lot of the big charities are suffering, through their relationship fundraising because the ROI on high value type fundraising tends to be lower than a mass event like A Race for Life or Macmillan Coffee Morning. And it is harder to find the right individuals for high value fundraising and it takes longer, it's not a quick win, but the long-term value's greater. And sometimes people aren't prepared to hang in, to wait, to believe in it enough.

Also in a small charity you can move quickly. You don't have to tick the box from the policy director and the brand director and then this team and that team and before you know it, you actually need to book out the board room just to get the new campaign or a new initiative through the channels to even get the business case approved. Bigger organisations I think are in danger of stifling creativity and innovation, just through their internal processes.

**Where do you think the next innovation in fundraising is coming from?**
When Movember first came and registered that was interesting, it was different, it was a movement. As was the ice bucket challenge and its use of technology but then everyone tried to get on the bandwagon and find an ice

bucket challenge equivalent. What interests me is where the driver comes from. Do the drivers always have to come from the charities? Or actually should we be more aware of and supporting the population and individual and society drivers?

## How would you define a successful fundraising team?
A successful fundraising team for me needs to know and understand the brand, the organisation, the cause. They need to be able to consistently give a coherent 5 minute elevator pitch about what the organisation stands for. They need to have real clarity and understanding, about what the organisation does, but also what their role is within it.

A successful team also needs to have licence to be creative, take their own initiative, take
risks. So I think, one thing that stops fundraisers being as successful as they can be is the, 'oh no, better not do that, because we haven't sought permission to do it' and 'well I'll go back and check with my supervisor'. Just be a little bit more ballsy, a little bolder. Be proud of what you do, have the confidence. A successful team always has confidence.

Fundraisers need to have the will to act on their own initiative and, I really think this one is really important, not be afraid or held back because they're think they will make a mistake and they'll be berated for it or that they'd have to explain it.

It's that freedom to fail. Because you know what, the worst case scenario, it doesn't work out then nothing lost, nothing gained.

## How would you describe your management style?
It isn't all my way or the highway. It isn't all about the director's ego, it is about positive motivation. It's give praise and credit, where credit is due, it's passing it down. Building that sense of team and talking the "I" out of it for want of a better expression. Succession planning is key and keeping people and building their skills and experience, I think you hold your workforce for longer.

But it's also taking the time to inspire and lead your team with your aspirations and your vision for the team. And also I think when you are in a more senior role it's important not to forget that you are also part of that team. I think it is a combination of how you set the culture of the team and that mutual respect, people having a voice, being able to listen. It's bringing them with you on the journey.

# LEADERSHIP INTERVIEW WITH KATE COLLINS

I've been lucky enough to work with Teenage Cancer Trust and have seen first-hand that there's something special about their culture. So it was great to have the opportunity to sit down with their Director of Fundraising & Marketing, Kate Collins, and talk about leading the fundraising & marketing team, retaining fundraisers and keeping the culture in times of growth.

With a background including BBC Children In Need and Cancer Research UK, Kate joined
Teenage Cancer Trust as Head of Regional Fundraising and has been Director of Fundraising since 2013, adding marketing to her directorate in 2014. Teenage Cancer Trust has shown impressive growth in fundraising over the past 5 years and has ambitious plans for the next 5 years too.

**The topic of my book is about leading successful fundraising teams. How would you define a successful fundraising team Kate?**
It's a fundraising team that's making the right amount of money for the organisation. And doing it in a way, and this is particularly pertinent at the moment in terms of in the sector, that isn't irritating people and is congruent with the values of the charity.

**Tell me more about how you go about doing that at Teenage Cancer Trust…**
I believe that a successful fundraising team needs to be really behaviourally aligned. But it's not necessarily about standardising everything. If you donate to Teenage Cancer Trust you might get a different 'thank you letter' depending on which way you give money to us but fundamentally you'll get thanked and you'll get (or you should get!) something that is friendly and warm.

What makes things work at Teenage Cancer Trust, might not work at another charity because their culture might not be as strongly driven as ours is by relationships, by being a family, by looking after each other, by teenage spirit and by eating far too much cake. **[Note from Carla – truly, in my experience there's a celebration involving cake at Teenage Cancer Trust almost every day]** In other places I've worked – and this isn't a judgement either way - some of the things that work here would be really weird behaviour, out of step with what those charities do.

So here a successful fundraising team is a team that really cares deeply about each other, cares deeply about supporters, that pitches in across teams, and celebrates success and has fun.

And actually playing and laughing is really important at Teenage Cancer Trust. We are a young organisation, we look after young people. And I would very much hope that we are raising money through relationships in a way that fits with the organisation.

**Your fundraising team has a lot of fundraisers working regionally. How do you keep the culture aligned and keep fundraisers motivated in those circumstances?**
Not always perfectly, would be what I would say. All my answers have to be qualified with that, that I haven't quite worked it all out yet and I'm not sure if anybody has. If they tell you they have, they might be stretching the truth. But when it comes to dispersed teams you need to deliberately engineer the things that happen more naturally when you're all working in one place. So when I was Head of Regional I spent a lot of time on the phone and I used to make sure that Fridays in particular would be the day I checked in with people. You phone them up and give them a space to download about their week or tell you about something they probably didn't think was exciting enough to email you about, but is something they really want to tell you about. Often those are the most important things.

It's also good to get people together as a whole team or as a regional management team and we find that arranging a creative session or a bit of an update session the day before allows people to stay over and be sociable. You have to be quite a lot more deliberate about engineering casual social interaction because otherwise it doesn't happen and fundraisers, I think by their nature, love contact.

**You work partly from home too Kate. How do you manage your time to make that work well?**
Since I became a director one of my learnings has been to understand what makes me productive in a different way. I've realised that actually being

good at my job isn't about strategies and budgets. Those are important, but those are almost the hygiene factors, it's kind of a given you can do those. It's all the other stuff, the soft stuff.

Because when you need to have a difficult conversation or something comes up that's a challenge within or for the organisation, that's when you need to have the bank of goodwill and trust and connection. And if you haven't invested the time in people to have goodwill in the bank, you could be technically brilliant but if you're on your own, it's pretty bloody lonely, and it doesn't work.

**I really like that analogy of the bank, that you're investing. You're investing in your relationships, you're investing that time in people and then that does come back to you. And if you haven't done it, you can't then go and ask them to go 'above and beyond' and expect them to pitch in. So, how does that work practically for you?**
I used to spend almost all my time in the office in pre-arranged back-to-back meetings. By contrast, today I've had loads of meetings, but many of those have been informal, unplanned conversations that have needed to happen.

And planning for informal interaction has become really important. I now give myself time in the morning to chat to people and I believe that a lot of my job is about relationships, connections and talking. If I look at my diary and think 'I've only got one meeting, is it worth going to London?' that's probably the day I most need to be in London because I'll get such richness of connection and conversation. What I shouldn't do is try to write documents on those days, because there's no point coming to London and sitting behind a closed office door.

Lots of people I work with also work from home or are on the move a lot, so I try and to use my at home time to do calls and get my head down writing reports.

**Tell me about one of your current challenges…**
For me the key challenge right now is all about keeping our fabulous culture as we grow. Yes, you know you've got to make sure the money comes in at the right return. But the team are really good at that. The team don't need me to worry about that. If they need me to worry, I know they will tell me to worry and when they need me to help me with that, they will pull me in to work with them.

So I think the biggest challenge right now for me personally is about not losing some of the intangible cultural elements of the organisation, the ones that actually meant that when we didn't have a complex formal strategy we were still doing a great job.

**So what are those intangible elements that you need to keep going? What is it that you think makes Teenage Cancer Trust special? Because I think it is very special in terms of its culture, having seen it from the outside and having experienced it from the inside as well.**

Well we do genuinely care and I think we as an organisation have been able to move quickly and change things in the NHS without actually ever being part of the NHS. So we've really embodied the ability to make things happen, even if we're not the experts in something. To be that really clear, simple voice for change. And I think we need to be very careful we don't lose that, as we're now moving to a place where we're working more in partnership with more organisations.

We need to focus on what makes us unique. Fundraising for a proposition around young people with cancer is attractive to bigger organisations than us. Bigger cancer charities than us are in that space with their propositions and big charities have more budget to spend and can afford to take more risks. Our approach is around personal relationships – we talk about our supporters being 'part of the Teenage Cancer Trust family' and you're more likely to get a hug than a handshake from one of my team.

I think we've got a quality that means our supporters feel like they've found us. And they like to tell other people about us. "Oh you really must get involved with them. They're really nice." That kind of endorsement is like gold dust and that's real return on engagement, not just return on investment.

**You talked about the engagement that your team have with the donors and a lot of that, I presume, is down to recruiting the right people or knowing what kind of people succeed at Teenage Cancer Trust. How would you describe your profile for a fundraiser at Teenage Cancer Trust? What kind of person do you want to come and work there?**

I think somebody who believes that fundraising can make a difference to the lives of young people with cancer and is hungry for and comfortable with accountability. Someone who is able to say 'yes I'll make something happen here, but also I'll be accountable for what happened if it wasn't brilliant and I'll learn.' Someone with a really curious mind who asks how they can learn and improve. You can't reverse engineer attitude.

And you need to be able to attract good candidates who will thrive in your culture – those two things are a rare combination. I've been quite deliberately making an effort (particularly after Stephen's Story because Stephen's Story is a remarkable story to tell) to speak at the Institute of Fundraising Convention and other sector events. Because it shows fundraisers who we are, what our culture is like and builds that broader sense of connection around our employer brand.

**How do you develop and retain talented fundraisers? Because a lot of fundraisers end up moving on for their next big opportunity, don't they? You've been good at retaining your staff, but how do you do it?**
Actually I'm re-reading the 'Happy Manifesto' by Henry Stewart at the moment and it talks about how, in order to retain people who are really good at their jobs organisations tend to turn them into managers, which they might not always enjoy and has a very different skillset.

So in terms of retention, I'd love us to be able to be creative and brave enough to have a path for people who are bloody good fundraisers and don't then have to become managers to progress or be recognised. I certainly look at my team and look at what they do and think 'you're an amazing fundraiser'. So it's a very current thing for me, thinking around 'how do we help people have more internal stretch and collaboration and be a safe place to learn?' And I think sometimes that within your current organisation can be the scariest place to learn, because you can feel so exposed. I think people sometimes feel they need to go somewhere else to do their learning. Reinvent themselves. And it would be great to not have to do that.

And I think, particularly with a growing organisation, it's about making sure we don't lose that technical brilliance. I categorically know I've got people here who are technically better than I'll ever be so how do we let them fly and know that they're making progress without having to move into management and away from fundraising?

# LEADERSHIP INTERVIEW WITH KATH ABRAHAMS

Kath has held a number of high profile fundraising roles including Development Director at NSPCC, Director of Engagement & Income Generation at Breakthrough Breast Cancer and now Director of Engagement & Fundraising at Diabetes UK. I interviewed Kath in early 2016 when she was 6 weeks into her role at Diabetes UK.

**Why did you choose this role and Diabetes UK?**
The cause attracted me. And the nature of the role. Diabetes impacts awfully on people's lives. Yet there is a really limited willingness to support financially and there's a limited understanding of the seriousness of the cause.

On the one hand there are 700 people being diagnosed every day with diabetes in the UK and it can have terrible health consequences if it's not managed properly. On the other hand, only 1% of the public see it as their most serious health concern. There's a disconnect there and we have the chance to help people understand the urgency and the seriousness of the cause. I also want us to give supporters an experience that makes them happy to be part of our family, and want to support us more. And for them to feel that we treat them in a way that they trust and is relevant to them and their experience.

I'm working with a CEO I've worked with before so I knew that would be a relationship that would work, and that he wants to build a culture that I want to be part of. Which is about empowering people, giving people responsibility for their areas, making sure people feel trusted. Safe to experiment. Free to get on with their jobs.

**What's the structure with your team?**
I've got 9 direct reports. The roles I inherited were 4 in fundraising and 5

who were in communications – the two departments are now one. I've got a Head of Major Supporters, Head of Community and Events, Head of Direct Marketing that covers legacies as well, Head of Fundraising Strategy and Resources, Head of Digital, Head of Media, Head of Marketing and Communications Planning, Head of Creative Services and Head of Brand. I'm very lucky. I've got a team of really experienced people who've got rich, diverse experience that they can bring to the table.

### What is your approach to the first 100 days in a Director role?
I suppose I've had the old 100 days piece in my head. That your first 100 days is the opportunity when you've still got fresh eyes. I think I start by learning and listening. Just asking lots of questions, but also making it really clear to my team from the start that I'm not interested in doing their job.

I develop my ideas through talking to other people. Building a sense of what I think about the situation, rather than coming in with a very fixed view. I've got some principles that I'd like to work. There's something also about making sure I don't wait too long and that I send some signals early.

I am now 6 weeks in and I've just shared my early thoughts about where I think we need to try and get to, both with our executive team, my fellow directors, and then my senior management team yesterday. I positioned it to the team very much as "Based on the conversations we've had over the last 6 weeks, this is what I think we need to be trying to do. Is this in the right ballpark?" It seemed to get a good read at first meeting. We're now co-creating the plan for 'well if that's right, then what are the big steps that we need to take to get there?'

Part of what I'm hoping to do here is empower my team as I firmly believe people are able to step up and take responsibility. That's generally what they want to do, and I know from my own personal experience, that I've performed best when I've worked for people who trusted me, rather than people who've controlled and questioned and limited what I'm able to do.

### Donor care is a hot topic right now – how do you make that feel personal in a large organisation?
I think some of it is about getting the basics of human interaction right. Everybody we're dealing with, however they support us, are all individual human beings. In the current environment that is rightly focused on compliance, let's also make sure that the relationships that people have with us feel authentic and that they can trust us. Many of our supporters either have diabetes themselves or it has impacted one of their loved ones. We absolutely have a responsibility to make sure their experience is one that

feels congruent and relevant.

## What sort of culture works best for fundraising in your opinion?

I'm quite a gut feel, instinctive person. I get a sense of culture by talking to people. By hearing the words they use. I like environments where people talk to each other and work together as a matter of course. When I first started at Breakthrough, I noticed people were sometimes emailing colleagues who sat opposite each other. That's the little stuff that I try and change.

Very early on I set up a fortnightly session here for just a half an hour where the team comes and just talks about what's going on. I knew the first couple would be a bit "tumbleweedy! The first one was people very politely being quiet, but all the other meetings since then have been people jumping and up and saying, "Oh yeah! Can I tell you about this thing that I'm doing?"

I love being surrounded by people who've chosen to do this because they want to make a difference in the world. I think it's brilliant that you have so many talented people who make that choice. Who are as professional and as brilliant and effective as anyone in the commercial sector. I also like the fact that generally, in the fundraising and communications world, people are hungry for success. I'm quite target and success driven actually, although I feel really strongly that there's one target rather than lots of little ones.

## As a Fundraising Director do you feel the pressure to increase income?

Sometimes it is a pressure. I won't pretend that isn't the case. But I think there is also is a very good understanding that we are in changing times. It's the same with lots of fellow directors I've spoken to.

It's the right thing for the sector to take a long, hard look at itself and think about how we raise money from the public. It's not knowing the impact that makes life challenging. You can do a certain amount of scenario planning, but ultimately we don't know what impact change will have on our income.

As an organisation, we absolutely need to look at how we grow our income. And it's clearly my role to lead on that, whilst recognising that without the support of the whole organisation, it's not possible to deliver it. We need to articulate better what it is we're trying to achieve. Prioritise clearly what we want to do and what we would do if we had more funding, so that we provide the environment for the public to get behind us and understand what we're seeking to do. All of which allows our fundraisers to go out there and inspire people. And we need to build great relationships that make people more likely to support us.

**How do you keep your team motivated and engaged in an organisation this size? The larger you get obviously the harder it is to have a connection with the cause sometimes.**
The first thing I'd say is I think that people here are already very engaged in the cause. We have a lot of people with diabetes who work for us. We also have a helpline and we have a lot of contact with people with diabetes. Having said that, I think there's always more we can do to help some people lift their heads up from the desk and think about the impact we can have and see the world from our supporters' point of view.

**How important are purpose and vision for fundraising?**
We're just developing a vision and mission for the charity. We see this as an absolutely critical thing to do. We want to articulate very clearly - this is our overall purpose and this is where we're headed.

Then we can take another look at our strategy in the context of the overall purpose and direction of travel, and the fact that diabetes is so relevant right now. We can look at how we maximise the opportunity we have to make the greatest possible difference to people affected by the cause.

**What about innovation? You increasingly see now organisations having innovation teams, for example. What are your thoughts on that?**
I think innovation is a bit of a buzzword. In the same breath I'd say it's one of the most important things that an organisation can do. If we aren't constantly thinking about what we could do differently and better, then ultimately our existing sources of income will just dry up. I think you have to nurture innovation in an organisation.

When I was at Breakthrough, we didn't have an innovation team but we developed innovation champions across teams. We did have somebody who was our innovation manager. Her role was to make sure that she was a catalyst, to help facilitate a process of innovation. I think in the case of Breakthrough we had lots and lots of good ideas but people didn't know where to channel them and how to get them off the ground.

Some of the process is around working out how you develop good ideas and how you make sure that people across the organisation can feed into that. How you channel them. How you test and learn things. How you take a little thing and do it and think, "Oh that works!" How you'd grow it. What's the investment? All of that. The nuts and bolts around innovation. Systemising it almost in a way that doesn't destroy the creativity but actually enables the creativity to happen.

## You've been doing this for quite a long time. How do you keep learning and challenging yourself?

I am still really interested in how things work. What makes people tick. How the world works. I like learning new things. I suppose part of it's a mindset. I find it fun. I'd get bored if it was always the same. I always know that I am going to learn from the people around me. I don't think I've ever gone into a new role and not had those moments where you go, "Oh! How interesting! I had no idea." I don't find it difficult to keep myself interested and engaged at all.

## What is the best thing about being a Director?

I love the breadth of being a Director. I love the fact that I'm in a role where I can link people up together. Linking colleagues up with our supporters and thinking outside-in rather than inside-out. I think you have to be comfortable with a certain amount of ambiguity. You have to like it, I think. If you want to live in a certain world, it might not be the role for you, particularly in the current environment.

I often have to give people the comfort and the confidence that it will be okay. Even though I don't know exactly how it will be okay, I do know it will be. It's navigating people through when actually everything around you is uncertain. People look at you to be the one that is upbeat, energetic, whether that's within the team or outside in the rest of the organisation. People want their Engagement Director to be inspired and inspiring. You need to bring that. You need to like that.

## What is one thing you've learned about leadership along your journey?

My first thought on that is there is obviously no single blueprint for being a leader. I think the most important thing is to be who you are. To be comfortable in your own skin, with all the shortcomings that that involves. To be comfortable in that space of thinking "I bring some things. I don't bring everything. Sometimes that will be the right thing for an organisation. Sometimes it won't be the right thing. That's fine." I think that helps me to be comfortable in a role that is full of ambiguity, and that has good days and bad days. That is full of successes and failures. To be able to say, this is the way that I'm going to lead people through that. That's the best I can do.

# LEADERSHIP INTERVIEW WITH MARK ASTARITA

It's not often that you get to pick the brains of one of the most successful Fundraising Directors in the UK. I first met Mark 15 years ago when he was leading the fundraising team at NDCS and I've watched him create impressive income growth and hugely successful and loyal teams at both NDCS and British Red Cross. Mark is Fundraising Director at British Red Cross and his team is 220 strong, excluding retail, and raised over £160m in the last financial year. With a stint as Chair of the Institute of Fundraising under his belt and never one to shy away from bold opinions, I was eager to hear what Mark had learnt about fundraising leadership in his years in the sector.

**You've been in fundraising a long time Mark and achieved a great deal. Did you have a master plan for your career?**
I've never been personally ambitious for myself. But I absolutely am ambitious for the organisations I work for or volunteer for. I get terribly passionate about them and really engaged in the organisational output and impact. It is never about the money for me. The money is just a mechanism for doing it, for creating change. And I think that's an important feature of great fundraisers - it is always about the difference we can make.

**How important is it for a Fundraising Director to have a clear vision?**
I think one of the things that great Fundraising Directors are able to do is to see a different future. Often they can see it before other people. It may not be well constructed and it doesn't have to be completely resolved but they are able to quickly adapt their thinking and their behaviour in order to shape their world and to be able to reach new goals. Some people let the world shape them, personally I could never be content with that. I think if you want to be successful it is fundamentally about mapping a wonderful future and then pointing people in the direction of how to get there. Not with every point on the map thought through, because you need other

people to help you do that. It is a collaboration of talent. I don't see myself as queen bee or the conductor of an orchestra where all do my bidding, more of a football manager constantly adjusting to the run of play.

I think great fundraisers operate in the future tense. The past is the past, this year is in progress and what we are going to raise next year and in future years is where I focus my attention.

## Does being so focused on the future create tension with other departments?

Many of my colleagues are rightly focusing on the present. Fundraisers are, by and large, planning, spending and operating in the future tense. What folk will give tomorrow was probably raised many moons ago. So I think we live in slightly different universes to some other parts of our organisations and because almost all our engagement is with the outside world whilst others maybe be more internally focused, we may see things from a different perspective.

I think at an organisational level, people can sometimes get a little bit annoyed with high performing fundraising teams, because they tend to all sing from the same song sheet. It doesn't matter which of my managers you speak to, they're all going to share the same vision and plan for the future. We swim as a shoal and that's quite a force actually.

We, and I suspect in many successful fundraising teams, see very high levels of organisational engagement in our people surveys. 90 plus percent engagement levels is not unusual because fundraisers understand the mission and strategy and interact with it every day. They can feel the way they can contribute and frankly they commit their all to the high goal. They tend to see things more from a collective point of view where every pound adds up to a greater organisational goal.

## So do you refer back to your fundraising strategy all the time?

I know some people refer to their strategy all the time, but it's not the way I operate. I almost always know where we are going, but I need to make sure everyone else knows where we are going too. So yes our strategy is highly visible but we tend to live and breathe it rather than use it as a totem pole.

People like to think it's all about the strategy and it's all written down like the gospel. I believe it's about having people who adjust daily, respond to the insight they gather and adjust to their environment. I'm surrounded by hundreds of years of fundraising experience. All my senior managers have been with me for nigh on ten years, and just get it. They don't make the mistakes that they did when they were a lot younger because, like me, they've already been there, done that and made mistakes in the past.

None of our great successes at British Red Cross were delivered by one big decision. It was more about the decisions being taken every day that myself, and my managers in particular, knew were the right decision to take that day and next week and next month. Cumulatively they add up to a big thing. So this idea it is one big thing bothers me. I think it is a product of our cumulative actions. Many of the things that have made the biggest difference grew from tiny shoots and featured strategically. For example, growing regular giving might be the big goal, but the path to that goal had many variations and products and not all were apparent at the outset.

**Do you think that as a large organisation with an established fundraising team that there's a danger of resting on your laurels?**
Oh goodness yes I hope we never do that. Needs evolve and for us human tragedy is forever unfolding. Being restful is certainly not part of mine of my colleagues' DNA. In our fundraising team we are always very aware that donors have got plenty of other choices for their giving. It's my colleague Richard Verden who always says, "We need to be perpetually petrified that people decide not to give to us."

There is something about that very forceful statement that no one has to give to us. Therefore we're always on duty, always in a sales mode. We've always got to be positive and we've got to believe in what we're selling to our very core. I hate the idea we are selling - it feels so tacky in some way because what we are promoting feels far more profound. I hope you know what I mean. My colleagues and I are ambassadors for our cause. So when people ask what I do, they are always interested in a way they would not be if I made widgets. Quite rightly, people expect the best of us all the time and we therefore have no excuse but to be 110% whenever we discuss our cause. Might be unfair after a long day but for me that is my reality. 24/7, always on duty.

The belief stuff is important to me too. If we don't believe wholeheartedly in what we're promoting, why should anyone else give to it? In fact why some fundraisers don't give to the causes they work for is beyond me. You've landed in a place where you passionately believe you can make a difference. As a fundraiser your beliefs, and why you're here are just as important as the aid worker or anyone else. You want to change the world, it's just that you've landed on the thing that you can do really well to do that. I'm not sure that is always as respected by people who aren't fundraisers.

### How important is it to have the right people on your team?

Our fundraising people strategy is that we are aiming to be the best fundraising shop in the sector. Known to be the best fundraising shop, where people want to come and work for us so that the fundraising brand is really powerful. We give people exceptional development opportunities, we grow exceptional talent and you know what? We know they will go, in time. Even after they've gone, we hope, they'll always tell others that they loved their time at British Red Cross. The fundraising brand grows as a consequence and we continue to attract talent.

Almost twenty of my former fundraisers have gone on to be directors of fundraising. That's the thing I'm very proud about. It's lovely that they think I was important in that because I don't always see it that way. I think they're all exceptional.

What really good leaders do is they do surround themselves with talented people. Talented teams are what create outstanding organisations. It is about creating exceptional teams and exceptional teams are built around a dream or ambition. They're built around a leadership style, a culture and that they all are sharing the successes. You don't nick all their success for your own. You celebrate their achievements and if you are lucky, it rubs off on you!

### How do you get the best out of the people in your fundraising team?

I think that ultimately the most important ingredient in running a successful team is about managing exceptional people and getting the most out of them by giving them extraordinary opportunities to stretch, hopefully in a supportive environment that never feels unsafe and that matters. People excel when they're in a space where it's exciting, interesting, fun and they're at the edge of the possible. We challenge people to be their best and we look to help them get there. There is not a lot of room for the mediocre in the teams I manage… heck it stands out a mile!

We've pretty much homegrown most of our first, second and third tier managers. Part of that is because there's nowhere else where you can do it as this scale or volume if you haven't done it in one of our four or five competitors.

In terms of team structure at British Red Cross, we have quite a steep pyramid. I have five or six people directly reporting to me, with steep pyramids underneath them. Second tier managers are my next level of talent. I'm always thinking about if someone gets run over by the bus, have I got someone there to replace that person? In the nicest possible way of course! I think I have five people who can replace me easily.

Another thing I think is really important is never to be fearful of your position. If you live in fear of your position, if you live in fear of your staff going to do you in or take your role then you're paralysed.

Personally I am an open book emotionally. I give of myself, am very loyal to my people and trust massively. I have in the last 25 years rarely been disappointed. I think I only do one thing really well and that is find great people to work with. Makes work great and rarely a chore.

**Any tips on keeping fundraisers motivated?**
Celebrate success. I know it's a very egalitarian sector. People say "Oh I don't know if I want to celebrate anyone over and above everyone else, everyone's contribution is important." I think we thrive on a bit of a pat on the back. As a workforce, I think, we're clearly not motivated by personal gain otherwise we wouldn't be working in the sector. That doesn't mean we don't love it when people applaud us for what we do and give us a pat on the back. Small amounts of effort going into that can be hugely valuable.

# ABOUT THE AUTHOR

Carla Miller is an executive coach and facilitator who works with individuals, teams and organisations who want to make more impact.

Her background includes leadership roles in the commercial and not for profit sectors as well as extensive experience as a coach, consultant and facilitator. She has been a non-exec director for two organisations and is a Fellow of the RSA (Royal Society for the encouragement of Arts, Manufactures and Commerce).

In the not for profit sector, Carla raised over £20 million for good causes, developed multi-million pound partnerships with blue chip firms and doubled income for a number of national charities. She then specialised in growth and change situations as an interim director and consultant.

Qualifying as a coach in 2008, Carla has been coaching leaders, facilitating team workshops and helping individuals develop their careers for the past 9 years. She enjoys helping clients to understand themselves and others better, uncover insights, discover useful tools and models and, of course, achieve impressive results.

Carla holds qualifications in executive and life coaching from The Coaching Academy and has undertaken substantial additional training as a Co-active coach with the Coaches Training Institute. She has also trained in NLP (Neuro-Linguistic Programming), Happiness Coaching (yes that's a real thing!) and workshop facilitation.

Carla is available for coaching leaders, coaching teams and facilitating away days and strategy days. She also gives keynote speeches on leadership and purpose.

www.carlamiller.co.uk
https://www.linkedin.com/in/carlamiller1/

Printed in Great Britain
by Amazon